LAND AND SEA

A Life in Politics and Real Estate

LAND AND SEA

A Life in Politics and Real Estate

James Vincent Fitzgerald

ATHENA PRESS
LONDON

First Published 2006 by
ATHENA PRESS
Queen's House, 2 Holly Road
Twickenham TW1 4EG
United Kingdom

Printed for Athena Press

To my ladies:
My wife and partner for sixty-three years,
Jean R. Fitzgerald;

My mother, Gladys E. Fizgerald,
for her strength and support

Thank you.
James V. Fitzgerald

Contents

Once Upon a Time…

Once upon a time, which is how a fairy tale goes, and I think it was a fairy tale for me when I look back…

My wife, Jean, and I were living in San Francisco. We had one son, and Jean was pregnant. We thought we couldn't get along in a one-bedroom apartment, so we should come down the Peninsula and buy a house. So we bought a house for $12,200 with $1,100 down and payments of $65 a month. It was three bedrooms, one bath and a one-car garage with a living room and a dining room. It was a nice location called Mills Park in San Bruno.

All the people in the neighborhood of about 200 homes were veterans who had come back from the war. They were raising families, similar to Jean and myself. They came from big cities in the East and from San Francisco, like I did. This little sleepy town didn't have all the amenities that they felt they deserved because they had all gone out and fought in the war. They wanted to become active and participate in the politics and government and make it a better place to live. I became part of this.

Family Origins

My father, James V. Fitzgerald, was born in Ireland and came over during the Potato Famine when he was two years old. He had six sisters and one brother. They all had typical Irish names like Molly and Nora, and so on. They landed in New Haven, Connecticut. My grandfather, whose name was also James, was an engineer on a train and was killed while greasing the wheels of the engine. The fireman backed the engine over him, cutting off his legs and causing his death. My father's older brother, Maurice, was about twenty-two at the time and was a purser on the ships that were bringing iron ore into the Great Lakes to make steel for autos at Detroit. He was so shocked by his father's death that he himself died shortly afterwards.

At this time, my father was eight years old. He worked at selling newspapers and his mother, Carrie, ran a boarding house for Yale students in New Haven. Everyone in the family worked after Father died. When my Dad was old enough, he went into the pharmaceutical business. In those days, the owners of drugstores made their own cold cream, corn plasters, toothpaste, etc., and put their own name on it. My Dad did that for a while, but he got tired of it, and took a train out to San Francisco.

He didn't know anyone in San Francisco, but he soon made a few friends. They told him that if he wanted to meet people – meet girls – the thing to do was to go to the National Guard Armory dance held every Saturday night. He went to the dance, and he thought it was great. He began thinking about joining the National Guard, and he took out an application. That night he saw in the paper that the National Guard was to be shipped to China because of the Boxer Rebellion. The article told that if the Chinese caught you, they cut off your ears and did all sorts of horrible things to you, including water torture. He decided he didn't want any part of the National Guard. According to him, he prayed all that night that something would prevent his going to

China. He decided to return in the morning and get back his application.

He was awakened in the morning with his bed moving from one side of the room to another. It was April 18, 1906. He checked in with the National Guard and found that he had not been accepted. He was happy about this because the Guard was going around with bullwhips and threatening to shoot looters, even if they were just getting food. He didn't like that at all. There was a big deal with Southern Pacific and the Federal Government to give free passes to get out of San Francisco because of the disaster, so he hopped on a train and went back to New Haven. Back in New Haven, Dad went into the chicken business with his brother-in-law.

They had these big incubators. The brother-in-law was to raise the chickens and Dad was to sell them. They had Rhode Island Reds. Dad would go into New Haven to the different markets and restaurants. They built up a fantastic business, making money hand over fist. Then the chickens got "the pits" which is a disease I have never heard of. Apparently, some bug bores into the chicken's head and it dies. So, Dad stayed up all night rubbing Vaseline on the heads of the baby chicks, trying to save them. In spite of all this effort, they lost a couple of thousand chickens. For a while, things were terrible. Then the tide tuned and they started making money again.

The next incident was an early snowstorm. The brother-in-law wasn't home at the time to bring the chickens in. They all piled up on one another for warmth and thousands of them suffocated. That did it for Dad. He decided that this was the end of the chicken business.

Things were better in San Francisco by this time. It was about six years after the earthquake and subsequent fire. Dad came back here, tried his hand at various things, and eventually went into the real estate business. In 1912 he had his own firm, Sunset Realty, located in the Richmond District. He was selling a lot a day, and had fourteen or fifteen salesmen working for him. When things got a little slow, he'd advance money to the men so they could live. Eventually they weren't selling anything, and he went broke.

Dad was a fantastic salesman, but he was not a good manager. He wasn't a good bookkeeper. He didn't enjoy those things. He went into business again with other real estate people and the same thing happened. He owned about four blocks in the Marina District when he and his partners got into a fight. They couldn't agree on anything, so they sold it all and ended up with nothing.

My father and his sister

Dad and I – Treasure Island

Mum and Sister Betty

My Early Years

I guess I should have started my story at 1927, because that's about as far back as I can remember correctly. We lived in the Galileo Court Apartments on Francisco Street, a half block from Van Ness Avenue, across from Galileo High School. I was about seven years old then. I had a group of friends. We called ourselves "The Gang" – Bobby Raggiotti, Ralph Cheli… I can't remember the names of all of them after so many years. The person who owned the Galileo Court Apartments was Ben Liebman. He was its builder. In San Francisco, in this area, you just run into people all the time. His son, Perry Liebman, was one of my big clients. I worked with him and his son, Brad Liebman. The son plays tennis down at the same tennis court that I do.

During W.W.II, Ralph Cheli was in the Solomon Islands. The Marines were getting the hell kicked out of them in Bougainville, down the Straits. The Japanese battleships would come every night. One night eight destroyers came down. Ralph was the squadron leader. His squadron attacked the ships and sunk or damaged all eight of them. This was the first victory of the war in the Solomons. At twenty-one, he was made a Major, and later on, after being shot down, he became the officer in charge of the Japanese prison camp at Rabaul Island. They shipped the prisoners back to Japan and on the way, an American submarine sunk the prisoner-of-war ship and all the people were killed.

You might say, as far as our economy goes, 1927 was probably the best of times.

I remember going around everyone's back door in the apartments and collecting Shasta fizz bottles and turning them in at the grocery store for 25 cents a bottle. I remember collecting a lot of bottles. I had so much candy that I bought Rough Necks and Home Run Kisses. These had pictures of baseball players in them, so I had a collection of pictures. The janitor gave me an old icebox that I had under the stairs, and that's where I would stash all my candy.

1924 – Jim, five years old

When things got bad and there weren't any bottles around, I could always dig in there and get some candy. During Prohibition, my family used to have parties; my father was active in business and they used to serve "bathtub gin". They'd take a gallon of alcohol and throw in some juniper berries and swish it all around to make this gin. Everybody would go nuts. A couple of drinks of that and you didn't know where you were.

About this time one of the teenagers, I won't mention his name, who was about sixteen years old – a tough guy – got another boy and me into his house to see his electric train. He tried to sexually assault me. I can't remember what actually happened in the melee. I guess I put it out of my mind. I know he broke my nose and I went home with a bleeding nose. The screwy thing was that I never told my parents. I don't know why. I had a bloody nose every once in a while until I was about seventeen years old. I knew what his name was and I watched him and thought about every alternative of what I was going to do to him. I figure that if you hate someone, all you're doing is hurting yourself. I just watched him. Years later his name was on a big sign at Market and Van Ness and I'd see it there all the time. I always knew where he was. Next thing I know I read in the paper that he was arrested and convicted for absconding with the company's money. As it's said, "What goes around, comes around". That was an excellent example.

Dad went to work for Umpsen, Kerner and Isaac as Sales Manager. They were a big downtown real estate firm located near the Fly Trap Restaurant on Sutter Street. He was doing real well.

We moved from Galileo Court on Francisco, off Van Ness Avenue. I was about seven or eight years of age, in the second grade at Sherman School. My parents bought a home on Broderick Street in the Marina District of San Francisco. I remember my mother telling me, "When you get out of school, go down Franklin Street to Chestnut. Turn left on Chestnut (to this day, I don't know my right from my left). Walk down Chestnut until you get to Broderick Street, then turn right on Broderick until you get to North Point."

We lived between North Point and Beach. It was the only house on the block, so I couldn't miss it. Believe it or not, I didn't get into any trouble and I arrived home – after some time!

Our new home was a nice two-story house. The area had been filled in for the Panama Pacific International Exposition, some time earlier. As a result, these lots had a lot of sand. My favorite pastime, I don't know why, was to dig down in the backyard and strike water. I'd go down, I used to think, about six feet. It wasn't really six feet, because I could climb out without a ladder. It must have been closer to three or four feet. The reason this interests me now is that later we owned an apartment house a block and a half away, at Divisadero and Beach Street. When the earthquake of 1989 hit, the buildings in the Marina shook, with some of them going down into the mud and goo. I remembered digging into the backyard and finding blue mud. That was the greatest thing for making mud balls. I got to know some of the kids in the Marina there, Bobby Watson and others, and we'd make mud balls.

Pretty soon they started building houses around us. One was being built right next door. One night I thought it would be good to have some slats that I saw over there. They'd be good for swords and my friends and I could bang each other around with swords. I took the clothes line down. I attached the clothesline and was hauling off those boards over the fence when the beam of a flashlight hit me. It was the owner of the house, who happened to be a lieutenant in the San Francisco Police Department. He talked to my mother. He wasn't too happy, but he was a nice guy, and she said she'd take care of the matter. I can't remember what she did.

One time the family of the police lieutenant started getting sassy and calling us names. We ran after them with our mud balls. We threw these blue mud balls all over the front of their white house! I can't believe what a stupid thing that was! Anyway, there was another knock on the door, and it was the lieutenant. He was nice enough to let me off the hook again. I don't know what they would do to me today if that happened. They'd probably send me away.

Another favorite pastime was to go over in one of the sandlots and play baseball with a broomstick and tennis ball. Sometimes, too, we would dig a hole and roast potatoes. They were probably the lousiest potatoes you ever tasted, but to us they tasted good, even without salt or anything else. It was just something we cooked up. We had a very interesting time and there was a lot of fun. Business was good; the family had parties and a lot of friends. Things were good at this time. Real estate was good, there was lots of food on the table, and we had no problems.

As I mentioned, this was Prohibition time. The Marina became a hub for the bootleggers, especially around the yacht harbor. The boatmen could bring illegal booze from Canada or other places where it could be made legally. Then the Depression came, and everything changed.

My Dad had paid $12,500 for the house, taking a $9,000 mortgage. One day he got a note from the bank to come in and talk to them about his loan. He knew he had a five-year loan. What he didn't realize was that it was renewable every year. He went to the bank, thinking that he had two years left on the loan. They informed him that they wanted to call in the note. He explained that he made his payments on time and his credit was good, so what did they mean? They said, "Oh, no, we're just calling it in."

He could pay off the loan if he wanted. He had thirty days to get someone else to loan him the money or they would foreclose. At that time, all the other banks were doing the same thing. The value of the house had shrunk to the value of the mortgage. Dad went around, but couldn't get the money to pay off the loan. We eventually lost the home by foreclosure: a nice, 3-bedroom 2-bath house, now probably selling for about $900,000.

We moved to the Chateau Marion at Van Ness Avenue and Greenwich Street that had just been built by a Mr. Arthur Rousseau. He was a very clever builder who did beautiful work, but he couldn't fill the complex because nobody had any money. He was a friend of my father. The rents were $500 per month, but my father could only afford about $150. Mr. Rousseau gave us a year's lease at $500, but we only paid $150 a month for it.

Arthur Rousseau was called "The Fox" because he had sailboats and he won all the championships racing in the bay. He had the *Ace*, the *Lady Gay* and the *Fulton G*. Those were all magnificent boats, especially *The Ace* and the *Lady Gay*. The *Fulton G* was more of a boat for you to relax on and travel, while the others were racing boats.

Then Mr. Rousseau sold the complex to a man named Burcott, who owned one of the best meat companies at the Crystal Palace Market. When Burcott owned the place, he looked at the leases and saw the rents were all for $500, but no one was paying that much. Everyone paid from one-third to one-half the amount. Rousseau did that to keep the complex full and allow him to sell it for the most money. There was a big argument afterward. I don't know how it turned out, but everyone moved.

We moved into a junky building at 2901 Buchanan, a block from Union. Besides my sister and me, we had a cousin living with us. She had been sexually abused by her stepfather across the Bay, and had been put into an orphanage. My mother brought her into our home. We had one bedroom, a living room and a dining room. Mom and Dad slept in the living room. I slept in the dining room, and Betty, my sister, and Marge, my cousin, slept in the bedroom. At that time I was just going into the 7th grade. I went to Pacific Heights School and eventually to Galileo High.

Things improved. We moved back into the Marina District and leased a flat on Beach Street right across the street from where Joe DiMaggio bought a home. Years later, when he married Marilyn Monroe, we saw him carry her across the threshold. After his divorce from Marilyn, he gave the house to his mother and father. That was a beautiful flat.

My father sold a piece of property, The Regilis Apartments, 350 units on Lake Merritt in Oakland. It sold for $1 million, which was an enormous sum. I guess today it would be worth over $50 million. The people, who bought the building, the Robson brothers, were real tough birds. They were multi-millionaires, but they said they didn't have the money to pay the commission, because it was too tight a deal. (This was a lie!) They also owned 145 Laurel Street in San Francisco, one of the nicest locations in the city. Senator Feinstein lives a couple of blocks from there now. At that time, there was a doorman and your car was delivered to the front door for you. The units had five bedrooms and four baths. It was a beautiful, elegant place to live. They offered us free rent there instead of the commission. We moved in and lived there for a couple of years and quickly used up the commission. The President of the American Trust Company and many civic leaders lived there and were our neighbors. I guess today, if they made condos out of it, each unit would sell for $1.5 million to $2 million. The location and the quality of the construction were just super.

Friends

During this fun time, I had a lot of friends, some that I still have today. There was Charley Ratti, who became the best suit man in San Francisco at Bullock and Jones. He had beautiful taste. My father always wore like a uniform a blue suit, white shirt and tie. Charley finally got hold of my father and got him into a sport's coat and slacks and a colorful outfit. When he went to Palm Springs and joined the Shadow Mountain Club, he felt just great. He would never buy anything unless he bought it from Charley Ratti.

Bill Schammel delivered papers with the help of my wife when they were both thirteen. He ended up selling 50,000 men's suits wholesale for all the famous makers – designer suits. He traveled all over Europe and had a wonderful life. He would go to the opera and sit in the Queen's box because he had friends in such high places.

Stan Jurvic was quite a guy and knew everything. He was in the clothing business when the War broke out and he became a bosom mate and they shipped him down to the South Pacific. When he came back, he went to work for Roos Brothers. A fellow named Gower that used to be head at Hastings decided to buy the Robert Atkins store. He and two others pooled their money, maybe $20,000 or $30,000, to buy Robert Atkins. Stan was the fourth man; he would be the manager.

When Stan's wife found out that Bill Schammel was making all this money as a traveling salesman, she got on Stan's case. She wanted them to go to Texas, where she was from. Well, this was a disastrous thing. They went through all their money and they decided to come back. They had no place to stay, so they stayed with us for about six months. Stan, Shirley and the two kids. Finally I got them a place in Stonestown. Fortunately, they took him back at Roos Atkins. While he was gone Atkins bought out the Roos Brothers stores. If he had stayed, he would have been way up in the company. They had about thirty stores by then. He was lucky to be the manager of the one that he originally worked in. One particular bum move, listening to his wife, meant that he never made the money he should have. She went to work and they ended up having a few cocktails every night, the two of them, and going out to dinner. Well, you can't accumulate any money that way. A war hero.

They all worked at Hastings Store and all went into the dry goods business later. My father didn't want me working like that.

There was Charley Leone, who lived on Octavia Street in Cow Hollow. His dad was a truck driver and the nicest guy in the world. They used to have a place in Healdsburg. In those days everything was shipped in boxes of knotty pine. Charley's dad would break up the boxes, and he built a house on the Russian River. He used to have all the kids up and he'd spend all day cooking. He'd have meatballs and spaghetti and salami and French bread. He must have been about 5' 6" and weighed about 250 pounds, and was a really nice, good guy. Charley took more after his mother, who was Irish. He went and worked for Pacific Electric. There was this great writer called Kathleen Norris. Kathleen Norris's brother owned Pacific Electric Manufacturing Company and it was very, very successful. She owned a lot of stock in it. She probably loaned her brother the money to get into it. Charley was doing well and he was the accountant for the firm. Kathleen Norris, I guess being an artist and being a really fine person, decided she'd sell her stock for par value. Well, par value was about $5 per share, and the market value was about $100 per share. So she said to the officers and to Charley that they could buy 5,000 shares if they wanted to and she would finance it. He could pay for the stock from the dividends. The dividends were 40%, and so in a couple of years he could own the stock. Charley fooled around and he was getting financing and he had the money. His mother-in-law would have given it to him, even though he didn't need it because it could be totally financed by Mrs. Norris. Charley was a very careful and methodical person. By the time he made up his mind, all the stock was gone and the 5,000 shares were immediately worth $250,000. So that was a bum mistake he made. Fortunately he came out of it and he went to a big company making plastics and rubber goods and became a vice-president and ended up with a very, very good retirement.

Bill Minnis was an awfully nice person. His father was head of the Fugitive Detail of the United States Marshal's Office and he was a real tough guy. He used to grab a fugitive and intimidate him. I guess today he'd be in the hoosegow if he tried that, but anyhow, he never had any trouble with the fugitives. Bill and I went on our first date together. He was dating Nancy Fay and I was dating Jean Rodegerdts, now my wife. Bill was a year younger than me, but he learnt to drive earlier than I did. At this time, which is amazing, the Mark Hopkins Hotel, the St. Francis Hotel, and the Fairmont Hotel had what you would call "representatives" at the high schools. The representative would be a classy guy and the idea was that he would give these coupons to his friends. With the coupons you could go dancing at the hotels and not pay any cover charge. You would buy a fruit drink that was $2.50 each, and maybe you bought your girl a corsage, at 50 cents. If she had two drinks, you never invited her again. So you sipped on that drink and danced every dance. This was the Big Band Era of Tommy Dorsey, Bennie Goodman, Freddie Martin – I could go on and on. It was so elegant and such a nice place to go. The waiters didn't push us. Bill and Nancy, Jean and I would go.

Charley Ratti loved beautiful ladies. He met this lady and I guess he didn't check her out or tell her what the deal was. He took her to the Mark Hopkins. They had a drink, and then she said she'd have another and then she said she'd like another. He said, "Excuse me, I have to go to the bathroom," and off he went.

Well, he lived about twelve blocks away, and he had to get some money from his Dad to pay the bill. I don't have to tell you, she was never invited again.

One time at Charley Leoni's place in Healdsburg we heard a black singer named Sanders King, who was unbelievable. They had big bands there, too. The blacks couldn't sing in the big hotels in San Francisco. There was a place called The Plantation at Fillmore and Sutter Streets. If you go down in that neighborhood today after dark, you could get killed. We used to walk from my house over the hills, down Fillmore Street to Sutter, and we'd go in and have a Coke. Everyone would treat us nice. We listened to this beautiful music and bounced home around twelve or one o'clock. We walked all the way and nobody bothered us. Unbelievable! It's so nice to think about how good it was in those days. Actually, at that time, nobody bothered the blacks. The only difficulties I remember concerned the Filipinos, who were having a problem because there were no Filipino women and they were going out with white women and some stupid, low-class people were competing with them for the women. There were a few incidents about that. Most of the Filipinos were working for the very rich people as houseboys and cooks and so forth. They were very neat and had fantastic manners. I used to play tennis with them up at Lafayette Park and they were great tennis players. I can't remember any bad experiences.

There was Walter Anderson, who came from Arkansas, and couldn't read or write. There was Ben Ichinose, who came from Hawaii. His grandfather had all the dealerships for General Motors in Hawaii, and they wouldn't allow him to become an American citizen. They wouldn't allow any Asians to become American citizens. So he took his family, except for Ben's father, and moved to Brazil.

Then there was Burton Miller. His father was a Polish Jew and was very frugal. It came as a surprise when Burt was a Junior in High School, his dad gave him an Oldsmobile convertible. It was a used car, but it cost $500, which today would be about $10,000. Burt decided we'd all go on a vacation and we'd rent a trailer. We rented a trailer from Happy Al's on Van Ness Avenue. Burt, Will Parker, Hank Hills and I were going to Lake Tahoe. We planned to leave at 4 P.M., but by the time we got the trailer packed it was 8 P.M. This was 1935. We left and got near Tahoe, I guess, when Burt ran over the railroad tracks. Will and I were sleeping in the trailer and all the dishes fell on our heads.

Anyhow, we had a marvelous time. We went to Reno and then ended up at Rio Nido on the Russian River, where all our friends were. This was a great gathering place where the big bands came, and you'd go to dances and you knew all the people. Prices were reasonable, too. You could buy a hamburger or hot dog and everybody was friendly.

Later on, Burt Miller owned the Regent Linen Supply Company. They made cooks' hats, aprons, and coats for people all over the United States. They had about 250 seamstresses. He had four children, and a couple of the boys have some of the nicest homes in Hillsborough. One is worth about five million dollars, and he's very well thought of in the Jewish Community.

One of my friends at school, Frank Pauson, and his father and brother, owned Kettleman Hills oilfields, and they were very, very rich. Frank's father was a real nice guy. He owned Pauson's Clothing Store. Frank always said that when we grew up, I was going to be manager of the clothing store. Thank goodness I never did become manager there!

We used to like to do things together. Frank's grandmother had a place outside Ukiah, in Redwood Valley, where Frank had a horse. Frank's father would buy him a new Buick every year and off we'd go to Ukiah. Frank would get his horse and we'd go to the neighboring farmers and Frank would talk to them for about an hour, and finally they'd offer me a horse. We'd pay for the horse and off we'd go into the mountains up near the Eel River. We'd be gone all day or stay overnight, and we'd see the streams and places and we'd round up some cattle. We had just a marvelous time. I came back regularly and pretty soon most of the farmers got to know me and freely rented me their horses. It was a kick. Frank, who was a very impatient person, was smart enough – very brilliant, in fact – that he knew that when you work with farmers, you never rush them! He would talk, and talk and talk about the hay fields, the crops, and all kinds of things that weren't about horses, and finally they knew what he was there for in the first place. They'd come out and say, "Well, would you like to rent one of my horses?" It was just a regular situation.

Frank's father had this house on Jackson Street that had about thirteen bedrooms. They had a Chinese cook, maids, and chauffeur – the whole works. Frank's mother was supposedly one of the most beautiful women in San Francisco. She committed suicide by jumping out of the window of their home. The father was left to take care of Frank. Mr. Pauson had three sisters. He invited them all to live in the house. Two were old maids, and one was married to Charley Tabor and had two children; so it was a pretty full house. The idea that Mr. Pauson was trying to develop was that it was a family rather than just the two of them living together. The interesting thing was that Mr. Pauson paid for a limousine and a chauffeur for his sisters and everyone else, but he took taxis every place because he said he couldn't afford a car – they were too expensive!

One day he told Frank that he wanted Frank to set aside Tuesday nights and they would have "school". "I want to talk to you about business," he said. Frank said he wouldn't go unless I could go, too. Mr. Pauson agreed and I went to business school every Tuesday night at their house. This is where I got a fabulous education. We would talk, for instance, about clothing. What was the best cloth? Was it flannel or worsted? Of course, it was worsted. I always remember what I learned there, and I've gone by these ideas like my Bible. One thing he taught me was that you don't ever lend money to a friend. If he's a friend of yours, you figure how good a friend, and you give him the money and don't think that you'll ever get it back. If they're a good enough friend, they'll pay you back. Otherwise, if you lend it to them, you're not only going to lose the money, but you're going to lose a friend if they don't pay you back. I've gone by this rule.

Another thing was never to own a second home. If you have a second home, everybody knows about it. They'll be piling in and your wife will be doing all the cooking and you'll be spending all your money. If you took the money you would spend on that second home and invested it, with the interest on that money, you could probably go any place in the world and you wouldn't have to go to the same place every year. I've gone by that and it's so true. There are so many things I learned from Mr. Pauson. He was a very, very nice man. I'm sure he was awful tough in business, but to us he was just great.

One night when I was there – this was during the Depression – a man came in and said he'd like Mr. Pauson to sign some hundred million dollar loans for the General Petroleum Company. He signed the loans and when the man left, Mr. Pauson said to us, "That man is going to go places." Well, that was Mr. Pauley. He has since become a billionaire. He donated the basketball complex in Los Angeles called the Pauley Pavilion, so he's extremely successful.

Another thing was that Frank's mother had two other children who were both girls. One had married one of the Fullers of the Fuller Paint Company. One day Frank suggested that we go up and see his sister. He had talked to her and told her that we'd be coming up. Well, they owned about 75,000 acres adjoining Lake Pillsbury in that beautiful country. They had their own airport and a complex of about three or four homes with a dining room over a brook with gigantic trout and oak shade trees and ferns and azaleas. It was just a gorgeous place. We went up and were assigned a cottage outside over the brook. I can almost hear the water now. That night we had dinner, and Frank asked his sister if he could borrow a car. When she asked why, he told her that she had a different car than his and he just wanted to try it out. She told him, "Sure, no problem."

We went out that night, out on the town. We went to Ukiah and we didn't know what the hell to do. We walked around a little bit and then hopped in the car and drove back.

The next morning at breakfast, his sister said, "You owe me $2.50."

Frank asked, "What for?"

"I looked at the mileage and know you went twenty-five miles; at $0.10 a mile, you owe me $2.50."

I couldn't believe it! Frank fished out the money; then she looked at me and said, "You haven't eaten your casaba melon."

I answered, "I don't like casaba melon."

She said, "That's no reason. You're wasting food. You have to eat your melon."

Now, this gal was about twenty-one years old and I was about sixteen at that time. Later we took a walk with her husband. He was a chemical engineer. We walked into the woods. The deer were popping out and there were birds. It was beautiful near the stream and I said, "My God, this is the most gorgeous place I've ever been; you must really love it here."

He said, "Well, I've always had it. I'm really more interested in my chemical engineering. That's more important to me than this."

The next day we went aquaplaning on the lake. In those days they didn't have water-skis.

They had their own polo field. There were always polo ponies, so we picked out a couple and went into this gigantic room. It was twenty-five by thirty-five feet and filled with saddles and mallets and all kinds of horse equipment. We hopped on the horses and Frank and I tried to play polo. We really had a good time. I guess my horse knew I was a green pea. I was ready to get on and he just picked up his hoof and stepped right on my toe. I looked at him and I knew he did it on purpose. They had this airfield out there and they used it to bring up the servants to Fuller's Ranch. Every week they changed servants. It was unbelievable. I don't know of any place around there that's like that today, where people can afford that kind of living.

Sometimes we would go skiing. One of us would drive for fifty miles and the other sleep in the back seat. Then the other would take over. We used to go to Yosemite for a day. We would start off at 4 A.M. and get to Yosemite by 10 A.M., ski all day and leave at 5 P.M. and get home by nine or ten. That was our system. One time a deer walked across in front of us. We slowed down and stopped and the deer dropped dead. We didn't want to leave it there, so we threw it into the back of the car. I wanted to take the deer to a butcher I knew, but since it was out of season, he wouldn't have any part of it. Jean, my girlfriend at the time, and I took the deer down Skyline Boulevard and dumped it down a ravine. We didn't want to get caught with it. We didn't kill it. It died and we just picked it up.

Frank Pauson was killed during WWII. His father had died and left him all his money about three months before he was killed. Frank was in the Navy. He was riding with a friend down in San Diego. The friend was going ninety miles an hour. The story goes that they hit a Coca Cola bottle and the car went into a tree and Frank was killed. This was a great loss to me.

I just thought of Carol Channing. When I was eleven years old, I went to a Christian Science Sunday School at the Church on O'Farrell Street in San Francisco. Carol Channing was in my class of six people for at least a year. The interesting thing was that her father was First Reader at the Mother Church in Boston, Massachusetts. He was like a "pope" for the Christian Scientists.

He was killed in an airplane crash. Nothing was ever said about her connection with the church.

I had a friend named Will Parker, and he was at school in 1935, 1936. He had flunked so many times; he said it took him six or eight years to get through high school. He was brilliant in his own way. We were in drama class together. We were in school plays, and our teacher, Hart Preston, was a *Life* magazine photographer. *Life* was very big in those days. Mr. Preston approached the *Life* people with the possibility of a spread in the magazine. They accepted it, and Hart Preston and Will Parker hitchhiked across the United States and had fourteen or fifteen pages in the *Life* magazine.

Will's mother had fled from Russia. She was sort of like an opera singer, a very beautiful woman, but definitely a pain in the neck. When we would go to Will's and she had guests, she would hide us in the kitchen because she didn't want anyone to know that she was old enough to have a kid our age. She went with the people from the Russian Ballet. Leon Mancine, I think is a name that I remember, was a great Russian ballet dancer.

Will's stepfather was an interesting man. He was a banker and worked for the Bank of America. At this time stock was low, and he came up with an idea he called "Time Trust". You could buy an interest of, say, $1,000 of Time Trust. This would be so many shares of Bank of America and Transamerica, and a life insurance policy from Occidental Life Insurance Company. You would pay, maybe, $25 down and pay it off over five or ten years, financed by the Bank, but at those original prices. You could be worth millions by then. He went through all this trouble setting it up and the SEC said he couldn't do it. It was almost the beginning of mutual funds.

I didn't know Will's father too well, as he was a reserved banker type and he didn't relate too much with young people. But he seemed like a nice person. He bought Will a new Ford convertible. Will got mad and ran away one time to the Russian River, but left the car at home. His father phoned me and asked if I'd help him find Will. He let me drive the car, which was an honor. We drove all the way to Russian River. There was Will, drinking a Coca-Cola. He didn't say anything, just hopped in the back of the car and off we went home.

When we were in school, Will was a great guy with the ladies. He had the Ford convertible. He had a bunch of silk handkerchiefs with a little perfume on them. After he took a young lady out, he gave her a silk handkerchief in a little box. They were crawling all over him. They thought he was the greatest. He was much older and more sophisticated than any of the other young males in school. He was quite a ladies' man.

Will was given a scholarship to Burlington School of Dance, and he met Carol Channing there. It was a college school to teach people to be actors and dancers. He was listed as an assistant teacher. Then he went into the Army and he was assigned to *Time* magazine to make some military films. When he left the Army, he had a business called Motion Picture, Inc., where he made movies for the Metropolitan Life Insurance Company, the National Real Estate Board, and the Bohemian Club. His stepfather was a member of the Bohemian Club. He always wanted to be in the Bohemian Club, but he couldn't get in as a regular member. There was a waiting list of fifteen years or so, but he got in as an artist and director. While he was in the club, he wrote the show *High Jinx*, which had about 200 to 300 players in it. He also wrote the show *Low Jinx* and the Christmas plays for the Bohemian Club. That was something no one else did. He was a fantastic as a director and as an artist.

Will was diagnosed with cancer, and his friends at the Bohemian Club knew this and had a luncheon for him. They had all the past presidents and vice-presidents and all the dignitaries of the club, which is considerable. They have all the biggest people in America practically belonging to it. He invited his friend Bert Miller and me as guests. They had a band and singers. They sang all the songs he had written for their productions. It was really a magnificent presentation of very talented people. It was probably never done before. Tears were rolling down from his eyes. On my way home with Bert Miller, we talked and hated to say it, but it was like his last rites or funeral. He died later on. He loved the Bohemian Club. He had all his time and money involved in the

Bohemian Club. He was in seventh heaven, and the closest thing to heaven was when they put on that luncheon for him and honored him. They just don't do that at the Bohemian Club, at least not for just anybody.

Let me tell you about San Francisco back when I was sixteen. We lived at Green and Buchanan, one block off Union. A friend of mine lived down the street. He was called Minori Lucca. Minori and I would take off in the morning before school and we would run up the hills on Fillmore Street, and go across town and run six miles out to the beach.

I belonged to the Olympic Club, and I used to go down there. They had a program and taught boxing, wrestling, gymnastics, swimming, fencing – all kinds of things. I met a lot of nice friends there. Frank Pauson belonged, and many other people I can't think of at the present. I played tennis. I had a friend, Carlos Stewart, who was a dear friend from age twelve. He used to beat me at tennis, and it drove me nuts. I thought I was better, but he was smarter. He had a sister, Gloria Delores. His father's friend was José Cansino of the Dancing Cansinos with Rita Cansino, aka Rita Hayworth, the movie star. Jose took eight years to make Gloria into the best Spanish dancer. She danced at the Coliseum, but then she fell in love with the drummer. She gained up to 200 pounds. What a waste!

I had a bad temper, which was why I always lost at tennis to Carlos. I had a big sunburn blister on my nose. One day "Spider" Roach, the boxing instructor at the Olympic Club, asked me to box Bob Bookey. He said, "He's slow, a 160-pound Stanford College boxer. He won't be able to hit you, you're so fast."

Well, we got into the ring and the bell rang. I went out dancing around, and he smacked me with a left jab to my nose. I got mad, losing all my boxing skills, and got beaten up badly. My nose was bleeding and my eyes crying. "Spider" said, "I would have stopped the fight, but you lost your head and got crazy." I have never lost my head like that again. It was the best lesson of my life.

There was a little guy named Whitmore Crow, and he was from Galileo High School, where I was going at the time. In those days, they had dances like the Debutantes' Balls. You were invited to come and you wore a coat and tie. You were to dance these dance school types of dances. I went to a couple of them, but we were not in the sort of society which meant I got invitations every week. I got an invitation from a lady, Eddynet Miller. (Crazy as it seems, my sister married Brunett Miller fifteen or twenty years later. He was a cousin of this lady's.) I knew what these dances were like, and I went to one with Frank Pauson. We climbed out the window and got the hell out of there, it was so boring. It was held at some fancy girls' school.

Whitmore Crow and some of his friends decided to go to one of these parties. They were going to get rid of the girls as soon as they could and then go to Dolly Fine's place. Dolly was madam of one of the biggest whorehouses in San Francisco. Whitmore's mother overheard them talking about what fun they were going to have. She alerted the police. After ten of them got down there, the police raided Dolly Fine's. Of course, they let the kids go, but poor Dolly was in a kettle of fish because they were all juveniles. They were the big men on campus when everybody heard. Everyone wanted to know which of the guys went to Dolly's and who didn't. Whitmore's father had a big business on Van Ness Avenue's Auto Row, the Crow Tire Company.

Early Business Experience

My father really loved me. In fact, he loved me almost too much. He had to sell papers when he was eight years of age. Even when we lost the house, he wouldn't allow me to sell magazines or take any kind of work. He wanted my life and my sister's life to be much better than his had been. We got into trouble when he concentrated so much on a large deal that he had. It was about $6 million or $8 million then, so you can imagine what it would be today, fifteen times that much. The Fox Theater at Market and Van Ness was one of the most beautiful theaters in the world. When you were in the top of the balcony, it was like 500 or 600 feet down to the stage. There were boxes decorated in gold. It was a gorgeous place. At that time, theaters made money. If you bought one, you could pay for it in three years. It was such a lucrative business because people were just starting to go to theaters because of talking moving pictures, and it was an outlet at the time of the Depression for fantasies in the movies. They made wonderful movies then and a lot of people went to them.

At that time, the young people like myself could get into the movies for ten cents. Warner Brothers, or one of those, Universal or MGM, was going to build a theater across the street. My father had worked a year and a half to get the options on the property so they could build. Finally, the deal did not go through, and he had spent a year and a half for naught and didn't make a nickel. That put him in real bad shape. That piece of property is now the site of the Merchandise Mart.

A lot of people today think the stock market's up and it can never go down. That time, when the crash came, the stock market people wallpapered their houses with stock certificates "not worth the paper they were printed on", as they say. A lot of people were really frightened of the stock market then. One fortunate thing was that my father had heard that Transamerica was going to go up, so he bought 100 shares at $2.00 a share, and it went up to

$7.00 – so he made $5,000. He was able to buy the property at 3701 Divisadero Street, the one that burned down in 1989. He paid $60,000 for that. It had sixty rooms, and when we sold it, we sold it for $1,800,000. The difference was great!

I was around fifteen or sixteen, and I had a job working for Erlanger, Reed and Meyer. I'd hop on the street car, go down to Montgomery Street and report to them about 3 P.M. and work until 5 or 6 P.M. as an office boy. There were about 175 different insurance companies around Montgomery Street, Sansome, Kearny and that area. I would deliver covering notes, binders, and temporary certificates of insurance. I'd pick up policies and do all kinds of running around, and I was getting at the end of the month $15. Sounds ridiculous – you can't get a babysitter to sit for four hours for $15.00 today.

It was an interesting experience and I knew where all the insurance companies were; I met a lot of people. It's a kick today when I go to the Fairmont Hotel to have my hair cut. Erlanger, Reed and Meyer are now Erlanger, Reed, Meyer and Dinner. Dinner is now an owner of the Fairmont Hotel because he married one of the Swig women. He was sitting in the barber's chair next to me not long ago and I told him that I was with his firm before he was and I told him, "You guys paid lousy wages." He wanted to know how much I got paid then and when I told him it was $15.00 a month, he couldn't believe it.

Russ Woldon was the assessor in San Francisco, and he was like a Robin Hood. He was supposed to assess all the properties at 25% of the present value, but he assessed the residences in San Francisco at 12% and then he assessed the business properties at 35%. Where he got himself in trouble was if the person protested, got to a friend of his, or gave him a little contribution for his personal use, he would reduce the assessment from 40% to 25% or even 20%. It was pretty well known at the time, and they finally caught him and sent him to jail. Years later, I took a tennis lesson from his daughter – Twinkie, I think her name was.

These times were tough. There was a general strike called. I remember that the Longshoremen came up Montgomery Street, and the Seamen's Union came up. Why they came up Montgomery Street, I don't know. They had uniforms. The seamen had white hats, and I forget what color the other groups wore. They all lined up, several thousand on each side of the street. You could have heard a pin drop, it was so quiet. They were just waiting for something to happen. They were threatening that this general strike would shut down all the food distribution, cleaning, banks – everything in the city.

All of a sudden, some black longshoreman, for some reason, ran out in the middle of the street, and all bedlam broke out. They were shooting ball bearings at each other. The police came, and boy, the police in those days! It took about forty minutes and then everything was back to normal. They didn't fool around and everybody knew they didn't fool around. I'm sure if you got picked up and hit a policeman, at that time you'd get the rubber hose treatment when you got back to the precinct. They did not fool around like they do today. Of course, I'm sure there was police brutality at that time, but the streets were safe and you could walk all over San Francisco any time of the day or night.

About 1937, I was graduating from High School, getting ready to go to college. I was supposed to go to the University of Oregon, but I was a poor student. I really didn't care about going to college, so I didn't go. This was a mistake.

At this particular time, my father was in business with a firm of Fitzgerald, Bonney and Traxter, down in the Alexander Building on Montgomery Street in San Francisco. They were doing quite well. We had lost our home in the Depression and we owed a lot of money. My father had just gotten to the point where we'd paid off all the bills and we were beginning to see the light.

In the real estate business, there are the listers who find the property and there are the sellers who sell the property and take care of it. Sometimes people want to do both.

In this particular case, Bonney and Traxter were "bird dogs", as my father caller them.

They were the greatest listers in the world. They'd list the property at the right price and they showed the property, and they brought the buyers in. My father was the closer.

He was a super, super salesman. I was in no way any where near him in selling. I was a clod. He was very good. The firm was making money hand over fist at that time. All of a sudden,

Bonney and Traxter came to my father, who was an Irish prima donna. He was about 5' 4" tall and about 125 pounds. They told him that they wanted to close their own deals. My father was livid because they had decided this without talking to him. He picked up his hat and coat and said, "Good-bye, gentlemen. I'll send for my desk and everything tomorrow." Off he went.

He had a big client, the Dorns. He talked to Douglas Dorn and they decided to have joint offices in the Russ Building. That was the time that I worked for my father. I drove him around, did various things, and eventually went into the business with him as the manager in his office, Fitzgerald and Dorn, in the Russ Building. I wasn't a good salesman. The uniform of the day was blue suit, white shirt, tie and hat. In the wintertime, the uniform included a dark overcoat. When I went there, I wore a blue suit, white shirt, conservative tie and homburg hat, and a dark blue overcoat in winter. Elevator operators ran the elevators at that time.

The Russ Building was the tallest building in town then, and we were on the 16th floor. We had a nickname – "The Gold Dust Twins". It was a great place to work out of, because if you were going to take clients anywhere, you phoned the garage and your car would be waiting. You did not have to park your car or anything like that. It was marvelous service.

The work I did for my father was as a sort of bookkeeper. I figured that it was silly that we paid rent of about $1,000 with expenses of $2,000. There was no way that we could afford being there, even though business was doing well. I discussed it with my Dad. He said he couldn't believe it – he never worried about things like that. My mother and sister really liked living on Laurel Street, but there was no way we could pay the rent there of $2,500.

We finally purchased the property at 2235 Beach Street, just half a block from where we had lived before. It had six apartments plus a penthouse. Each apartment had 1500 square feet, doweled maple floors, cathedral ceilings, pedestal basins, stall showers and canvas walls. It was half a block from the Palace of Fine Arts. We bought it for $350 down and a mortgage of $36,000, which was $10,000 more than the property was worth at that particular time.

My mother and sister were mad at me about moving and banished me to the laundry room on the roof. Today each unit is selling for $450,000.

I remember we had a deal when we were in the Russ Building there with Douglas Dorn of Dorn Properties. Douglas was interested in buying the Crestview Apartments, which was at the corner of Washington and Gough Streets. I think there were over 100 units there. They had a marine view and it was a beautiful building. We had a contract to sell it for $1 million. The seller was not that much interested in selling it, but he signed the contract for thirty days. Douglas Dorn didn't have $1 million, but he had five apartment buildings: one at 1060 Sutter Street, one on Jones Street, one at California and Gough, one on Eddie Street. My father started working on this and when he concentrated on a deal, he really concentrated on one. He sold all the properties within thirty days, and he had the deeds and most of the money was in the title company.

My dad's favorite bar was on Bush Street. He'd give the piano player $20 and the piano player would keep playing the "Polonaise". If my father had one drink, that was the end of him. He couldn't handle his liquor too well. He was a very nervous person, but a few drinks like that kept him out of the booby hatch because he was a high-pressure worker.

He figured the deal was closed. I received a call from Douglas Dorn and he said, "Jimmy, get up to my office immediately." He said the deal had gone kaploohy. He told me to go get my father. He was at "On the Hill"; that was the name of the bar. Dorn said to get my father and this deal back. Stewart, the owner of the property, had just received a $1.5 million offer, and we had only until 5 P.M. tonight or the thirty days would be up. If we didn't close the deal tonight, it would be off.

I went up to "On the Hill" and found my father sitting at the bar. He asked why I was there. I told him the deal was going kaploohy and Douglas Dorn says, "Get off your tail and get down there and get the deal back together."

My father said to tell Dorn to go jump in the lake.

I asked, "Aren't you coming?"

He said, "No," and I knew it was no use arguing with him

because he was a little stubborn. I went down to see Dorn. I told him my father said to go jump in the lake. He laughed. My father could say anything to him, but I couldn't. Dorn told me to go get it fixed. I went down to one of the escrow companies, a rival title company. I found out that we were about $20,000 short. One buyer needed $20,000 and it was not going to be at the title company until Monday. I told them the commissions run about $30,000, so why don't I just defer the commission until Monday so that the loan can go through. They thought that was a good idea.

I went to the other title company and told them to do that. The title went through that day, barely one minute before 5 P.M. The deal went on record, and my father gave me $5,000. That was what was used to put the down payment on a house in San Bruno. It was an interesting time.

Sally Stanford was a tenant of Douglas Dorn. She was the biggest madam in town at the time. She catered to all the big wheels. Just about six or eight months ago, I ran into Louie Zellerbach Seroni. When I was a kid, in my school, we had very rich people: the Zellerbachs of Zellerbach Paper Company, Haases of Levi Strauss, the Pausons who owned Kettleman Hills, big clothing people like Ransahoff, and Roger Boas. It was an interesting time.

Louis Zellerbach Seroni was telling me the police were always trying to raid Sally Stanford's place. She had her place fixed like a castle with a moat and you could hardly get in there. One time, Roger Boas was there when the police tried to break in. Sally put him in the closet. The closet happened to be where she kept all her best booze. It was a rainy night and Roger had his overcoat on. He figured this was a pretty good deal, so he put a couple of bottles in his coat. After she had saved him, he had taken off with some of her booze.

She phoned Louis Seroni and said, "You get that jackass back here with my booze or I'm really going to fix him."

Roger became City Manager of San Francisco years later. He was indicted for child molestation just a few years ago.

The interesting thing about San Francisco at this time was that my father knew Roger Boas's father, Nate Boas, and his uncle.

They were known to be some of the forty thieves in San Francisco. You couldn't borrow from a bank on an automobile then. You had to go to places like Boas Motors and they would lend you the money at 13%, 15%, or 20% – as much as they could get. They were big wheels and they eventually owned a lot of property and a lot of the whorehouses in town. They made a lot of money.

Douglas Dorn was the nephew of Sarah Dorn, who was a descendant of a Spanish grantee who had extensive acres of land in the Sonoma area. My father had sold some of this land to various people. He traded it, mostly, for apartment houses in San Francisco. These apartment houses were some of the best in the city. The Francesca Apartments are right in back of the Fairmont hotel, and 2210 Jackson Street. I'm sure that one would sell for seven or eight hundred thousand dollars if they were converted into condominiums. There was a piece on Sutter Street. He had about ten pieces of property worth millions of dollars even in that time.

Douglas Dorn was about thirty years old at the time. He was a horse's ass, as far as I was concerned. One day his mother and his sister and brother were in the office. He called me in and asked me to get a statement on the Brocklebank Apartments. I got the statement for him. He asked how much it was. I told him, "Well, the price of this particular property is $1,500,000."

He took the statement and says, "That's ridiculous, don't bring me anything like this!" Then he threw the statement on the ground. I had to pick it up. I said to myself, I can't believe this. I'll never, ever work for just one person again in my life. I never have.

I had to get my real estate and my insurance licenses. My father was a good friend of Louis Lurie, who later owned the Giants baseball team and sold it for $100,000,000. He owned the Mark Hopkins Hotel and a couple of skyscrapers down on Montgomery Street. He was about the same size as my father. His office was in a penthouse, on the 33rd floor, of 333 Montgomery. I went up with my father. He'd always want me to go with him and listen, and later when we came back, he'd ask me to tell him if he did good or bad, or what. We were up seeing Mr. Lurie about buying some piece of property. Mr. Lurie said to me, "Jimmy, I tell you what. You get your insurance broker's license, and I'll give you a million-dollar policy."

I was nineteen or twenty then, and boy, I went out and studied and studied and studied. You know, at the time, stenographers were making $65 a month! And they took shorthand, and typed and were super-looking people. I passed the insurance broker's license and I already had my real estate license.

I went flying up to see him and he wasn't there. I made eight or nine trips and he was always out or too busy. Finally, I guess he got tired of thinking up excuses to avoid me, so he gave me two tickets to the Curran Theater! That was my first lesson in life. When I think back, Mr. Lurie did not have any obligation to do anything for me. What he did was stimulate me to do better and to get my license quicker, which was to my benefit. But in my way of thinking, I never want to ever say anything or make a promise and not fulfill it.

When a buyer came in for a piece of property we had advertised, my job was to take the buyer through the property and show it. If he was interested in making a deposit, my father would take care of the signing and negotiating with them. I would type out the papers and take care of going to the Title Company, doing the escrow work, and so forth. I had studied the broker's test on real estate. I had my driver's license since I was sixteen, so I had been driving people around for my father since then. I had driven San Hamburger, a former barber who had become a multi-millionaire, the Anexters and the Fleishhackers. All these people were tops in the city, because my father handled big apartment houses.

This was 1937–8. We had 150 buildings for sale by the San Francisco bank that we could sell for just the mortgage and our commission. There were so many foreclosures it was unbelievable! It was hard to find anyone with $2,000 or $3,000 to pay half of our fee for selling the property. Everyone who we sold property to at this time became very wealthy.

A lot of property, just like my father's, was taken over by the banks. Dave Blain would find an apartment house with maybe 100 units. The owner wanted, say, $1 million for it, and there was an $800,000 loan and the best offer was probably $600,000.

So, the owner had no equity. The bank would have foreclosed on the $800,000. Dave Blain would say, "I'm going to give you $5,000 and you give me a quitclaim deed to the property."

The owner would think this was great. He owed money and couldn't sell the property at a price even close to the mortgage. He would take the $5,000 and give the quitclaim deed. Dave Blain would call the bank and tell the president or top guy that he had a 100-unit apartment. He would ask if they were interested in buying the stoves, linoleum, fixtures and carpets. The guy at the bank laughed and said they were going to foreclose on the property and take it over. He thought it was a joke.

Dave Blain would then get a bunch of guys to come in and take everything that was not nailed down: fixtures, stoves, refrigerators, everything. When the bank foreclosed, even though the stuff wasn't worth much, they had to buy all new items. The banks would go deep in hock. Dave tried this several times, so pretty soon the banks learned. In the future on property loans, they would get a bill of sale and a chattel mortgage to take care of the property on the premises that was not attached to the building.

I decided that I was going to be an entrepreneur. I sold a piece of property and I made a $500 commission. Some people we were working with who represented San Francisco Bank loved to have cash and they saw I was going to get $500. They said, "Jimmy, we've got a 14-unit apartment house up here on Clay and Baker, near Presidio Avenue. It's got two threes and twelve four-room apartments. It's about $45,000. The $500 will take care of the down payment and you just have to pay the installments to the bank."

Well, it was about 50% empty. I think the rents were something like $50 a month. First thing there was an explosion in the hot water plant and it was like $1,000 to fix it, and I didn't have the thousand dollars, so I lost the apartment building. You didn't have any money. Nobody had any money. Those were some of my experiences that I had in the real estate business.

When we bought the property at 2235 Beach Street, we weren't making much money, but my father could see that things were starting to pick up. When he wanted to buy another piece of property, the bank president, Parker Maddox, said that if we bought another piece of property from the San Francisco bank, the bank would foreclose on all our properties. This is how powerful the president of a bank was in San Francisco at that time. He ran the city with Harry Bridges and a couple of other people. It was a tight ship. Everyone jumped when he said jump.

Harry Bridges was a very powerful labor leader in San Francisco. When he took over as president of the Longshoreman's Association, he had strikes. He was active in trying to have the general strike in the city that I mentioned before. He did succeed in raising the wages of the Longshoremen and he brought a lot of the minorities, especially blacks, into the organization that were barred before (I'm not sure abut the Chinese or Japanese). With all these new members, he was able to stay in control for a long time.

In around 1988, I had lunch with J. Hart Clinton, publisher of the *San Mateo Times*, who was an attorney with a very powerful firm in San Francisco – I can't remember the name. He was a negotiator for some ship owners. He was the opposite of Harry Bridges. He started to tell me what happened. Jimmy Hoffa, the notorious leader of the Warehousemen's Union, and I don't know what the heck else, came out to organize and get a contract with the shipping people in San Francisco. He was a powerful person. He talked to Hart Clinton, and Hart Clinton said to him, "We want to work together and get a rapport so we can finish these labor negotiations as soon as possible." Jimmy Hoffa said, "Listen, I'm going to tell you what to do, and you are going to listen to me, and that's the way it is going to be, so you may as well figure that's it."

Hart Clinton did not particularly like this. He was sort of a tough guy, too. He went to Harvard Law School and was a publisher of a paper, a real prima donna. If you didn't know him, you probably didn't like him. When I didn't know him I didn't like him. When I knew him, I liked him very, very much.

All of a sudden, there's a strike. Hoffa's people had pickets around all the ships. They were very active, and all of a sudden the ship owners started talking to Hart Clinton. They said, "Hey, we'd better sign a contract with Hoffa. He looks like he's the most powerful, and we can't go on much longer with this strike. We've got all these goods rotting here on the beach, and we've got to get it moving."

So, Hart Clinton decided to go over and see Bridges, but Bridges wasn't there.

Lou Goldblatt was there. He was sort of the number two man. Clinton said that they were going to be signing with Hoffa, "If you guys don't show any power, it doesn't look like you represent all the Longshoremen. It looks like Hoffa does."

The next day, Hart Clinton said he saw about ten of these big flatbed trucks go out with guys with baseball bats and cargo hooks. They went out and just tied into each one of these pickets and knocked their heads in and cut them up with the cargo hooks. It was a slaughter. All kinds of people were injured, but the Harry Bridges group was able to clear away those pickets and maintain their power. They ended up getting the contract and Jimmy Hoffa didn't. It is frightening to think about the way they used to operate, when Hart Clinton would tell me something like that.

World War II

I was the manager of the insurance business. Doug Dorn was so afraid he was going to be in the Army because war had been declared in Europe that he decided to take out a $1 million life insurance policy from me. This was an enormous policy at that time.

We talked after he finally was sober enough to pass the physical test. They had to send his urine analysis back four or five times before he could pass the test to get $1 million. He drank about a quart of Scotch every day and he was thirty years old. He asked, "Do you know why I bought this policy?" I said I didn't know why he had bought it. He said me, "Prudential Insurance Company is certainly not going to let me get in the front lines, because they would lose $1 million."

I thought to myself that he was supposed to be such a smart guy, but I didn't think Prudential gave a damn whether he was in the front lines or not. I didn't think he would ever pass the physical to get in the Army, Navy, or Marines.

Before the war broke out, I decided to sign up for the Naval Intelligence, which was called the D.I.O. (District Intelligence Office). It looked like there would be war. I submitted my application and started to close down the insurance business. Then I waited to be called. I found out that it would take six months to a year before they finished checking on me. In the meantime, I decided to go to work for Bethlehem Steel Works. I became an aide to the Superintendent of Engineering in the shipyards. They were building ten destroyers and five cruisers. My job was to fill out the progress reports on engineering. I kept track of such things as how far along were the boilers, etc., in each job and when they would be completed.

When I arrived at the Superintendent of Engineers' department, a very nice man, Mr. Holmes, warmly welcomed me. He was absolutely busy. There was a war going on in Europe, but we weren't in it yet. Of course, we were delivering supplies to Britain and we were losing ships. We found out that we didn't have a very modern Navy, and this is the reason we were building these ships at Bethlehem Shipyard. The superintendent said that he had to know what the estimated completion time was on each piece of machinery in the engine room. He also needed to know the progress of each individual piece. This was like talking Greek to me, because I didn't know what kind of machinery he was talking about. He was busy interviewing "inside machinists". These were the people with the technical skills to build the parts he needed You couldn't just buy these parts; you had to make them.

I learned about economizers and boilers and condensers and all kinds of different things. I asked one of the assistant engineers, and we made a list of the different items in the engine room. After fighting with the superintendents inside each ship, I finally did arrive on some estimated times for each piece of machinery. There were fifteen different ships to keep track of. I got 4" by 4" pieces of accountant's paper with lines going both ways. I put the name of the ship on top and the list of components. The dates were shown across the top. A blue line going out showed the estimate for each item for each ship. A red line showed the actual progress. Every morning I put these fifteen pieces of paper on the engineer's desk at about eight in the morning and then I'd pick them up about 9:30. Then I would make my rounds again. Then I became more sophisticated. If something was going as smoothly as possible or if the superintendent of a job would tell me that no part was available or so forth, I attached a note stating this.

I was there six or eight months while the Navy, FBI, and Army Intelligence were investigating me. Finally one day I got a memorandum that I had been accepted to the United States Naval Intelligence Unit, and that I was to report within a week after I cleaned up my business. I went to see Mr. Holmes, who hadn't said more than "Good morning" to me in all that time. He never complained about anything and never said anything good; he was just busy. When I went in and told him I was going to leave he almost had a stroke and said, "You can't leave! You're indispensable!"

I said I was going into the Navy. He said, "I can get you a release, because we need you here."

I said that I didn't know that. He said the sheets of paper and notes had saved him months of work. He said it was so simple he could look at the paper and tell where everything was. I told him I was sorry, but I was not getting drafted, I had volunteered for this and had given my word.

"You have been very nice. Thank you and good-bye," were his final words.

The United States was not in the war yet, so I went down and reported to 717 Market Street, the Kamm Building. I was assigned to the A-3 section and went to work. I got my uniform, but I was living at home. Four or five months later, I went out with my future wife, Jean, and we stayed out late. I was sleeping in that Sunday, and I woke up and heard that Pearl Harbor had been bombed. All ships, sailors, and all men were to report to their stations immediately. I was in shock; I went to see Jean and told her that I had to report, and she wanted to know what was happening. I said, "I don't know what's happening and I don't know what they're going to do with me. I'm in the Navy, so they can do anything they want."

Jean's mother was pretty nice. She fixed me some pheasant for lunch, not knowing when I was going to get back. I went down and reported. I hopped on the "F" car down to the SS *Kamm* and reported in. We then took the necessary steps in getting the information on the various suspects whom we were working on so that we could turn them over to the FBI. They were to be rounded up so precautions could be taken to ensure there would be no sabotage.

They stuck me in the night shift, and Jean thought that was a great idea because I could work at night and then we would have all day long to go to the beach or do whatever we wanted. The only trouble was that she forgot that I had to sleep. I'll tell you, I had never been on a night shift from midnight until eight in the morning and then tried to get some sleep. If you are not used to it, it's awfully difficult. I can't remember why, but they moved me back to the day shift and I became in charge of my particular department. I had over one hundred people working for me – many of them outranked me. It was a crazy Navy. I never went to boot camp, didn't know what the Navy Manual was, or a damn thing. Neither did anyone else in our organization.

The pressure started building up and so forth, and I was just twenty-two at the time. I was pushing everyone around to get them to do more work. There were some pretty smart guys there, and they tried to figure out a way to sabotage me. I was a Third Class Petty Officer and under me were First Class and Chiefs. In the Navy, that just isn't done. Third Class Petty Officers don't order Second, First or Chiefs around. Of course, not being a Navy person, I felt I was in charge and that was just the way it was. There was a war going on and we had work to do.

They kicked me upstairs, and then I was checking the work, which was a much easier job. There were no problems at all. The person who took my place, Bill Breen, became the vice-president of personnel at Bank of America later. There were some real sharp people there. Ed Williams was under me, and he ended up the managing partner of Stone and Youngberg; that is a multi-million dollar outfit. He was a good guy.

After the war had been on for a few months, Jean and I decided to get married. We went to Yosemite for our honeymoon. We were married on April 11, 1942. We rented an apartment from my mother at 3701 Divisadero for $30 a month. That was at the corner of Divisadero and Beach. It was what they now call a studio. We called it a two-room apartment, when it actually had a living room and a closet. We slept in the closet. It was a big closet.

I told them I'd like to be shipped out. Everett and Bert Wines and Murray and Caselli and a few of the other guys said there were some openings and they wanted to be shipped out, too. They shipped us out to Hawaii. We were at sea for six days and there were about 4,000 men on the ship. The bunks were four high. I had the highest one. The Captain told us before we left to stay in the middle of the ship: "Get as much fresh air as you can and eat as much bread as you can and don't look at the horizon." I did all these things he told us to do. I volunteered as a lookout. I was watching for submarines and, of course, I had never been to training and wouldn't know what the heck anything would look like. I was out on deck and it was interesting, but it was cold. I had my pea coat and a hat on, so I was warm enough. Finally, at two in the morning, I hadn't been relieved, so I asked permission from the bridge if I could get a relief. I looked around and everyone was

Jim and Jean's Wedding Day

sleeping down below. I saw some guy who was a seaman first class, and I was a third class petty officer, so I tapped him on the shoulder and said, "You are wanted on the watch."

He said, "I don't feel like going."

I told him it was an order. He got dressed and went up and took my place watching. I don't know what I would have done if he hadn't done it.

The next morning when I woke up I had to go to the bathroom. I went in and it seems all 4,000 of the young people had been sick in the bathroom. I never saw such a mess. All the desire to use the bathroom went away and I went to get some air on deck. They gathered up all the seamen to clean up the mess. When it was cleaned up, I went down to take care of my private business.

We arrived in Hawaii. They placed us in Pearl Harbor, but when we got there they said they didn't have room for us. They suggested we go out and get an apartment or some other accommodation. I guess we were non-combatant people, so they wanted to get rid of us. We went out and rode a bus and looked for apartments and couldn't find anything. In those days, it was "Sailors and dogs keep off the lawn". Another thing was, enlisted men couldn't buy hard liquor. You could only buy it if you were an officer. An interesting point! We finally talked the bus driver into renting us a room in his house. We rented the room, I think, for $60. At that time it was an enormous amount of money for one room.

All our uniforms were dirty after the trip over. We were supposed to report in the next day in our whites with shoes shined and in first-class condition. We washed the uniforms in an old washing machine. We spent the night washing and ironing. We arrived the next day at downtown Honolulu. We worked there in the day shift and soon they asked me to take the night shift. I took over the night shift; I was making about $120 and I think about $50 subsistence, and any money we could get Jean was putting away. She was trying to live on the salary or whatever I sent her.

Our next apartment was three or four blocks from Waikiki Beach. It was a junky place, but at least it was a place we rented and the three of us could live in it. There were cockroaches and other things, so every Sunday we'd take the furniture out in the front yard and wash it the place down to kill all the bugs. This upset the owner a bit. Two guys worked the day shift and I worked at night, so they gave me a car to come home because there was a curfew. I would drive the car home and then they would drive back to the D.I.O. in the morning.

I was walking down to the beach one day, and this guy said to me, "Hey, got anything to do?"

I said, "No."

He said, "Want to rent surfboards?"

I said, "Yeah."

This was the Army Rest and Rehabilitation Center and he had his own surfboards. I would go to the beach around nine in the morning after getting home from work at 12:30 or 1 A.M. I would rent surfboards for him until 3 P.M. and then go to work at 4. At that time there were only about three hotels on the beach. There was the Moana, the Royal Hawaiian, and the Halekulani. It was very peaceful, and the Hawaiians still fished there with their nets out all night long. The Hawaiian ladies in their muumuus would collect seaweed, which I never tasted. Sometimes the Hawaiians would go out with a sling gun and bring in a small octopus. It was really the best time to see Hawaii.

This guy had his own surfboards, and he didn't want to get them mixed up with the Army surfboards. They were long boards, about ten or eleven feet. He'd put them on the beach, and I'd rent them out for $1 an hour. Finally, Naval Intelligence found out I was doing this, and oh Christ, they really raised holy hell. They told me I couldn't do that kind of stuff.

Then I decided to go out to the University of Hawaii and take a couple of courses. One was Economics, but I don't remember what the other one was. I did that for a while.

There was an unoccupied Coast Guard building with some barracks. They decided to put us all in the barracks at the immigration station in Hawaii. We lived there and had our meals there and lived like real sailors. We had been spoiled because now we had to get permission to go out on Saturdays or Sundays, as we were on duty all the time.

Before, when we were on subsistence, we had our own place and could come and go as we felt like.

I was able to get out and see different parts of the island. It was very beautiful and interesting. When I got home I told my wife about it. Naval authorities forbid me from asking her to come over during the war, but sixteen years later, on our twentieth wedding anniversary, I took my wife and three children to Hawaii.

We were over there for about two years when the war ended. One of our roommates was Johnny Wynn. On the day of the cessation of hostilities in Europe, Johnny's wife was crossing the railroad tracks in San Carlos, in San Mateo County. People started blowing their horns because of the news. She thought they were honking at her and when she went to cross the tracks, the train started up. It hit her car and their baby fell out and was killed when its head on the steel track. This was a real tragedy that we lived through at that time.

I didn't meet Robert W Salles until I was about twenty, I guess. He eventually married Claire Tarpey, who was my wife, Jean's, best friend. When I went to Hawaii in the Navy and was gone two years, Jean and Claire lived together. Bob Salles went to France and he was a sergeant in the hospital division, or whatever it was. When he and I came back we didn't know what we wanted to do, and at that time we were both married. Bob worked for Tidewater Oil Company and was sort of a clown and was drinking. I thought, Well, you know, he wasn't very conservative. Of course, I guess I wasn't either.

Anyhow, he went to work for Claire's uncle, Paul Tarpey, at Paul Tarpey & Company. Actually the company was just one person. He'd been in the wine business, inter-winery sales, for about twenty or thirty years. He was an honest man, but he wasn't very aggressive. He made friends, but he didn't make very much money. He could go to see any of the wine company people, Marquis Dupens, the DeMartinis, and various others.

He took Bob with him, but he wouldn't let Bob make a sale until he learned every kind of grape and all the different elements of wine. He taught Bob about the alcohol, the acidity, the color, and the various different things. They would sell maybe a hundred thousand gallons of wine to one winery because the color of their red was sort of pink, and they wanted to buy a heavy, deep color wine to mix in to come up to their standard in color. Sometimes, the same thing would happen with alcohol, if their wine was eight or nine per cent and they had to get it up to twelve per cent. They had a nice little business going, and it got better and better. Finally, Bob didn't like the way Paul was handling him, or he didn't feel he had enough freedom. He said to Paul, "I'll tell you what. I'll give you $1,500 a month for as long as you live, and I'll buy the business."

Well, $1,500 a month at that time, my God, was a lot of money. So Bob went out and made friends with the Gallos and the DeMartinis and the Wentes and all these different people, and he treated them all alike.

One time, he told me, Gallo phoned him and asked what the price of Cabernet was a gallon. Bob said that he had four hundred thousand gallons of it and the price was 90 cents a gallon.

Gallo said, "Oh, I can buy all I want for 70 cents."

Bob said, "You goddamn lying no good dago bastard, don't give me that crap. You can't buy any of this wine at this quality for that kind of stuff."

After that, they became good friends. When Bob died, I was one of the pallbearers, and Gallo and DeMartini and Wente were too. They were all saying, "Now who have we got that we can phone up like the New York Stock Exchange and find out what the price is of Cabernet and what the price is of the various wines in any winery?"

This was the wholesale price, of course, before it was finished. Bob became very, very wealthy.

Home Again

We came home from the war. The thing was, what kind of business was I going to go into? Naturally, I felt I would continue in the real estate business. Downtown offices were expensive. We thought the people we were working with would never come to our offices there. We decided to put an office in at 3701 Divisadero Street and work out of there. We worked there and sold a lot of property. We got some interest in various properties. I sold a chicken market in Oakland, and was supposed to get a commission of about $2,500.

My father's associate, Edlin, a fellow from Realty Liquidators, heard about it. He needed cash just then; everybody needed cash. He wanted to grab the fee and close the sale. He said that for the $2,500 we could have a quarter interest in a 30-unit apartment house at 3018 Mission, plus the corner plot. A Mr. Guppy owned another quarter interest, and Byron Arnold and Edlin owned the other half. (Byron Arnold was an attorney who later became a judge.) Of course, it had a $100,000 mortgage even though it was across the street from Sears Roebuck.

That's where that money went, and we got a foothold in that deal. Then Edlin wanted to sell his interest. Dad borrowed $10,000 from Guppy. He ended up with a half interest in the Mission property and Guppy held the other half. With the $5,000 Dad had put down on the 3701 Divisadero Street property and its twenty-one units, we had both properties in the family.

When I was in Hawaii during the war, it was apparent the Big Five controlled everything. If you were fired by C. Brewer & Co. or by Hawaii Sugar Planters Association or Castle & Cook or any of those groups, you couldn't get another job on the islands. You may as well get off the island.

When I was in Hawaii, I met Jack Hall, who was a lieutenant to Harry Bridges, and a fellow named Reinecke, a professor at the University of Hawaii. They were complaining that the sugar workers and longshoremen were not getting the amount of money they should get. They were getting about $3 a day, and one day they came in and demanded to get $10 or $5 an hour, I forget. Anyway it was certainly much better. The trouble was that the Big Five in Hawaii did not like minorities. They didn't marry blacks or Asians, and so forth. They were a bunch of snobs. The minorities couldn't go dancing at the Royal Hawaiian Hotel. Whites ran the whole thing.

Jack Hall married a Japanese gal, Yoshiki, and then Reinecke married a Chinese gal. There was another guy who married a Korean, I think. They started organizing all the Asian groups. When they had an election, they became head of the Hawaiian sugar union and the labor union for the longshoremen and warehousemen. Of course, they raised the wages, and everyone thought they were the greatest things since Swiss cheese.

Years later, I met a lady from Washington who was part Japanese. It turned out she was the daughter of John and Yoshiki Hall. She wasn't too happy that I knew so much about her. She had married one of the Burton brothers who became a State Assemblyman. Jack Hall and Harry Bridges had put their organization behind the Burtons. Later he divorced her. When I met her she had a good job, so maybe she wasn't so unhappy.

When I was in the Navy in Hawaii and the war ended, I was offered a job at $500 a month, which was really unheard of at that time. I thought about it. I had been on the island for over two years. I had good times, but the island had become small. I was not "in" with the Big Five. If you weren't "in" with them, you would never move into the higher echelon. You wouldn't go to the country clubs. You would not be acceptable. I turned the job down.

When I came back from Hawaii, my father had been doing business with the Emmicks. Gene Emmick was the head of Golden State Theaters, or something like that. They owned eighty-nine theaters in the State of California. They owned the Mid-Town, the Uptown, the El Rey, the El Capitan, even the El Camino in San Bruno and on and on. My father was buying property for them for new movie houses. He was also buying property in areas where movie places could be built, just to keep another movie house out.

John Saul, who was the real estate man for them, was making about $100,000 a year. He was getting lazy, so he was letting my father do some of his work. He planned to retire, so my father thought this would be a good job for me. He arranged for me to have an interview with Gene Emmick. I knew the family well. I knew Clarence, his brother, who had bought a 30-unit apartment out at 101 Point Lobos Avenue, near the beach. I knew Grace, his wife, and Retha and Clelta, his daughters, and Harold and Walton, his sons. I knew them all well. As a matter of fact, I had dated Clelta. She was a very beautiful girl, but I didn't want to get into any trouble because her family was a customer of the firm, and we couldn't afford to lose any customers at this time. Clelta eventually married a doctor and Retha married a naval officer.

I went in to see Mr. Gene Emmick at the Clay Jones Apartments, and we got to talking about the future. He was a man of about eighty and he had his girlfriend there. I think she was about twenty-eight. After she left we started talking about the future. I think he was in bad shape. All of a sudden, he got off the subject and said, "They are building these televisions. I think television is going to grow and there will be these big clubs, like the Bal Tabarin (which was a big club in San Francisco). They will have a big screen and people will go and be able to eat and look at this television, a movie on television."

He was a little worried about that, but he felt it was the way it would be in the future. He kept talking like that. He said if I wanted to work for him, he would give me $500 a month. I thought about it. I had worked for Douglas Dorn, and I knew what a pain in the ass he was, and I had made up my mind I was never going to work for just one person again and have all my eggs in one basket. So I told him I was not interested.

About six months later, he sold out to Naify, who had a small interest in the operation. Naify bought all the properties. Naify, his son, is listed now as being worth $1 billion. There would have been no way for me to get any place in that organization.

Old Gene Emmick was right. He had enough foresight to know that television was really going to affect the theaters. They changed the whole way the business works. In his day, when you bought a theater, the profit was so big you could pay for that theater in three years.

The Emmicks were the most unforgettable people I have ever met. I'm still in contact with them. Grace was a former school-teacher and she was a very intelligent lady. She was very lovely and attractive even at about sixty-five years of age. She had bought and sold gold, back in Paducah, Kentucky. Gene and his brothers, Clarence and Lauren, were from back there, too. Grace told me a story after we'd become friendly, about when they were on the river back there. She heard rumors that the Emmicks had this fancy apartment in Louisville, or someplace in the South. It was very fancy, and everyone was talking about it; they all had their girlfriends up there. So Grace said she got a couple of Negroes (as she said at the time) and a couple of mules and a big wagon and went to Louisville. When she got there, she opened up the door. Clarence drank a quart of whiskey in a day, so when he was drunk, she had gotten his key and had a copy made. She went in and found all this fancy furniture, silverware, booze, and every damn thing. She took it all out and put it in the wagon and drove back and put it all in her house. Nobody said anything about it. She was a real character.

Clarence loved to buy property, so he'd call us. My father said he was half deaf. My father would tell me to show him some motels. So I took him down and showed him a bunch of motels and he bought the Lindy Motel in Salinas for about $150,000. He stuck Grace in there to manage it. They have a Rodeo every year there in Salinas, and a lot of people look for rooms, and in those days there weren't that many rooms. Grace would rent out the chairs in the lobby. Not only that, she rented out the rooms in their three-bedroom house next door, and even rented the kitchen. She then slept in a wheelbarrow, at seventy years of age. She was incredible.

One night, after about six months, Grace called me. My wife had just had an operation and was recuperating at home. It was about nine o'clock when Grace called and said, "Jimmy, come on down. I think there is a man interested in buying the motel."

So, we hopped in the car and drove down to Salinas and wrapped up the deal that night. She told us we might as well stay over, and said I could sleep in the living room. There was a big bed in the living room. So Jean and I went to sleep. When we woke in the morning, there was a line to the bathroom. We didn't realize that she rented out the whole place. There were cots in the hall, and we were sleeping with all these people we never knew or had seen before. Grace was really something.

She made $40,000 net and she made another $75,000 on the sale of the property. We went up to the city and looked at a piece of property on Geary Street with a couple of penthouses on it. I took her through and we were all ready to go to the Title Company. I always check to make sure the statement I give the buyer is correct. We went over the information, but the seller had given me information that was not correct. It was about $500 or $1,000 less than the information I had before. I had to go back to Grace Emmick and tell her she could back out of this deal because the guy had misrepresented it to me. I said, "It doesn't add up to the income I told you that you would get."

She said, "Jimmy, I said I was going to go through with the deal and I'm going to go through with it."

I asked her, "Are you sure?"

She said, "You heard me."

I told her we were going to need to get some money and go to the Title Company.

She asked if I would help her with the money. I said I would. We went into the closet and there were some bags. She said they were silver dollars. There was $27,000 in silver dollars with $1,000 in each bag. All I could carry was $2,000, about 120 pounds. Trying to get rid of those dollars was like getting rid of a body. The Title Company would only take $5,000 of it because there was sand in the bags. Finally, we were down to the last $5,000, and I remembered an old friend from the Navy, Buck Tremly. He was manager of the American Trust Company at the corner of California and Fillmore. It wasn't the greatest neighborhood in the world, there was no parking place and I had this $5,000 in the car. I parked in a red zone and told Buck I had $5,000 in silver dollars. "Will you help me out and take them?" I asked.

He laughed and said, "Jim, you are a character. Sure, bring them in."

So I brought in the sacks of coins, and he couldn't believe it. No one else in the bank could believe it, either. He did me one helluva favor. We were about $27 short, so I had to come up with that.

Another character I met was Sol Boboir, who was one of the people who bought a piece of property out of the Douglas Dorn deal on the Crestview Apartments. He bought the property at California and Gough. He bought it and paid $250,000 for sixty units and sold it to the Lerner people, who owned the Lerner Shops. He made $50,000 profit in about ninety days. Sol was a plumber. He did not know anything about the real estate business, which was to his favor.

At this time, all the smart guys, like Louis Lurie, Sam Hamburger, and all the rest of the brains, weren't buying property because the prices had gone too high. They didn't think it was a good buy. Sol didn't know this, and started out buying an $8,000 home in the Richmond District and then the next week he sold it for $9,000. He thought this was pretty good, better than plumbing. So the next week he bought two houses, one for $10,000, the other for $11,000. He sold them in a month or so and made another couple of thousand dollars. He was buying and selling a couple of properties every week. He was having a ball.

Finally, we had this piece of property we were having a terrible time selling. It belonged to Dr. Francis Quinn. It was across the street from Lafayette Park in Pacific Heights. It was about eighty units. We had it up for sale for about $180,000. I thought I would try to get Sol; he might like this property. Maybe my father told me to do it. I went and showed him the property. He thought it was all right and offered $145,000 for it.

I went to Dr. Quinn and told him I had an offer of $145,000, and Dr. Quinn said he was not interested. He said he would take $145,000 net, which meant there would be no commission involved. I went back to Sol and told him if he went to $150,000, we could make the deal. He said he really didn't like the place that much. He said, "How about going to lunch and having some fish. Do you know of a good place?"

I told him I belonged to the Olympic Club and I invited him there.

We went to lunch. I offered him a cocktail, and we had a couple of Manhattans. I ordered the fish, and the Olympic Club had the finest food in town. After we finished, he said, "I'll go $150,000." So, I made $5,000 on that lunch.

I asked Sol why he was doing this, and he said, "Well, I've always been a plumber, taking care of toilets and the rest of the plumbing. It feels good to get up in the fresh air and have a nice lunch with you." That was how we made the deal.

He used to carry around $40,000 to $50,000 in cash. Some real estate man, I don't know who, told him there was a big piece of property down in Merced or Stockton, someplace. He went out to look at it. It was a ranch. No one ever saw Sol since. Some people thought he ran away from his wife, but nobody knows to this day. At least, I don't.

San Bruno

To get back to 1948, Jean and I had a child, Jimmy III. She was pregnant with Chris, and we decided we must have a home. We had come up in the world from my mother's studio apartment at $30 to a one-bedroom at $45 per month. Now we went to a three-bedroom, one-car garage, and one-bathroom house in Mills Park, San Bruno. Veterans were given home loans at 4%, so with $1,100 down, our mortgage payments were $60. This was a big stretch for us. Shortly after moving there, Jean had to have an operation. She had developed cancer of the thyroid. She was pregnant, and her gynecologist found a lump on the side of her throat. He said she should take care of it when she had a chance. Jean, being very practical, said that as long as we had insurance, she might as well take care of it right away. I cannot emphasize enough the importance of insurance. Since this was not within a gynecologist's specialty, he asked who her other doctor was. When she was young, Jean had stitches in her leg for an injury playing football. This was done by a Dr. Yank Chandler, so she gave his name. In the meantime, he had become head of Stanford University Hospital, then in San Francisco. That operation lasted five hours. She later had another operation done by Dr. Victor Richards.

There was a five-year period when she was not "out of the woods", so to speak. We are talking about over forty years ago. There was no chemotherapy, and the knowledge of how to cure cancer was very limited. Any time someone had cancer, you wondered if that was the last you would see of them. Although she wasn't supposed to, Jean got pregnant again with Suzie. We were very fortunate, because she recovered, and we had the three children: James, Chris, and Suzie.

During this five-year period, I was not doing the real estate business in San Francisco, selling apartment houses and flats. Jean needed attention, both emotionally and physically and everything, so I moved my office from San Francisco down to San Bruno to be close to her.

The closing of my real estate office in San Francisco was a staggering blow to me as I had really been involved in the real estate business in San Francisco since I was eighteen years old. I knew the vales of almost all apartment properties in my area, but Jean's cancer was a bigger problem that needed to be solved.

I probably would never have gotten into politics but after five years, the cancer was in remission and Jean was functioning well. I then had a chance to get into another career.

I specialized more in the insurance business, because with real estate, you have to work nights and weekends. She really needed someone home at night and on weekends. I closed my real estate office in San Francisco, unfortunately, I was a real estate person, not an insurance expert.

We belonged to the Mills Park Association. We were all young veterans who came out and bought these homes in 1948. It was a very civilized area, like San Francisco used to be, but there were some problems. We were upset because the water was so hard that it made deposits in our pots and the water heaters were being ruined because of these deposits. We organized the Mills Park Association to address these problems. They made me a vice-president. The reason I became vice-president was because I didn't want to do anything. I did not want to get involved in something like this. I did not want to talk to people or make speeches or anything. I just opened the door and made arrangements for the meeting places and things like that.

After a couple of years, they wanted to have an election. They said they had to run somebody against the current president. I told them I didn't want to run. They promised me they wouldn't vote for me; they just needed an opponent on the ballot to make it look legal. It ended up that I won the presidency by one vote! The rats double-crossed me.

We then got involved in a campaign to have the city build a gigantic water softening treatment plant so that we wouldn't have all this hard water. It was hard to wash clothes, and it made these deposits that ruined water heaters. By gosh, during the campaign, everybody got involved. It was a $1 million bond issue, if I remember right. We had 62% of the people in San Bruno vote for it, but it took 66½% to pass. It's a good thing it didn't pass, because if it did, San Bruno would have been broke. Also the water softening process isn't good for some people with heart conditions, etc.

We needed more room, so we moved into a place on Redwood Drive. It was three bedrooms, two-bath house with a two-car garage, and Jean hated it. So we moved again, to a place at 109 Crystal Court in Parkview Terrace. This house had three bedrooms, two baths and hardwood floors. We added a rumpus room later. We paid $21,000 for this house, with $2,000 in extras. The house was built by Alfred Hansen.

Hansen built a lot of houses in Parkview Terrace. We got to know him pretty well. I was selling lots and anything I could. I got a listing of five lots in Crestmoor. I took Alfred up to look at them, but he said they were terrible; he wouldn't have any part of them. I suggested he build an apartment house, but he didn't want any part of that, either. I kept going back to him saying that there must be a way. Finally he said he would go in it if I went in 50-50. He said, "You get the financing and the loans, do the management and maintenance and operation, and I'll do the building."

So, he started building. He wanted to do the job right, which is the right thing to do. We wrapped the pipes so there wouldn't be noise and we had floating ceilings so the noise would be less. We galvanized pipes and steel beams and supports in the garage. All that ran up more expense; we each had to come up with another $20,000. I think we owed about $500,000. We had about $100,000 in it, $50,000 each.

More Friends

Andy was another close friend of mine. I met Andy through Pat, a good friend of my wife's best friend. He came from Arkansas, supposedly, when he was sixteen years old. He didn't have any money. He just walked into a place that was a body shop and used car dealer and started sweeping the place out. He popped in the car and went home with the owner. The owner asked where he lived and Andy said, "I live with you. I'll clean your house and cook for you; the place looks a mess."

He did, and learned the car business, too. He was doing really well, just doing repair work. He decided he'd sell old Cadillacs. So he started selling Cadillacs, and met this Joe Conforti, who owned two legal whorehouses, one in Reno and one in Las Vegas. Andy sold him four or five used Cadillacs. Conforti would take the girls and exchange them. They'd be at the place for a little while in Reno and then he'd drive them down to Las Vegas and vice versa. So he'd put on these miles and he'd bring the cars in and Andy would fix anything that went wrong. He had Joe's complete confidence. When the cars wore out, he sold them some more used Cadillacs.

I guess some of these girls had pimps. The pimps wanted Cadillacs, too. So he started selling cars to these pimps and whores. He had a deal with them: "You pay so much down and $200 a month" – or whatever it was. It was due by 5 P.M. on the 30th of the month. If it weren't, he'd take the car back. So he got a bodyguard, a big guy named Cerrini. He was about 220 pounds, a real tough guy. I guess they kept a duplicate set of keys, so that if it was the 30th, and the guy didn't pay the money, they'd go out and find the buyer. If they didn't find him, they found the car and brought it back. If the guy tried to hide the car, Andy had a deal with the police. He'd give them $100 cash if they would get the car because he'd say the car was stolen because they hadn't made their payment. You can't do that today.

He developed a big, big business and made a lot of money. After the War he got his hands on a lot of brand new Cadillacs and he sold them at fantastic prices, because you couldn't get them. Then he got a dealership for the Volvo Company.

Bob Salles became good friends with a fellow named Bill Bagby, whom he met during the war. Bill met Irene Nicolai. Her mother, Natalie Nicolai, was a fugitive from Russia. She was one of the White Russians, a Tartar or part of the Czar's family, I guess. Her husband was a colonel in the Cossack Army. She came to the United States with all kinds of diamonds tucked in places where the Customs Officials at that time didn't look. So she ended up selling beautiful designer clothing to Magnin's and other stores. They were doing well and bought a place in Hillsborough. It had about twelve bedrooms and it was on a several acre lot. They built a tennis court and gorgeous swimming pool and big cabana with a bar in it. It had a changing place for men and one for women and it had a dance floor. It was absolutely beautiful. Irene married a man named Earl. Earl worked for Irene's mother and they lived with the Nicolais and they had a spending allowance of $800 a month and nothing to pay for. They had three children and a governess and maid. They really lived it up.

Andy lived next door, and apparently he was up on a hill. One night his Cadillac went racing down the hill. Earl saw it. He rang the bell and said, "Your car has just gone down the hill and crashed into the woods."

Andy said, "Forget it, I'll take care of it." He was eating a can of beans, cold. He was in an ugly mood.

Earl finally asked Andy to come on over, and they became friends. They used to have these fabulous dances and parties and everything. Andy met Pat Janeau there and ended up marrying her. That's how I got to know Andy.

They bought an apartment house in Burlingame on El Camino. He tore out a couple of apartments and made a big apartment. He put mirrors on the walls and all kinds of fancy, glitzy things and it was really beautiful. He liked antiques, and he had many beautiful things. He had a knack for buying antiques as an investment. He just had the smarts. After that he bought a forty-foot yacht, and it was beautiful. It carried about 600 gallons of gasoline and it had two bedrooms and two bathrooms. He put it over in Sausalito. It took him about a year to train me how to run the boat. Even though I had been in the Navy, I didn't know anything about boats.

One day he phoned me and said, "I've got some people coming from Sweden, Volvo people, and I wonder if you could come to lunch and meet them."

I went and met them and we went to lunch and then he said, "Do you mind? They're a drinking bunch and I have to join them and I can't drive the boat. Could you drive the boat?"

So I said, "Sure." I was driving the boat and Andy was the bartender and we had all sorts of hors d'oeuvres and so forth and they had a great time. He entertained them for a couple of days and afterwards I said, "Gee, this cost you a lot of money." He said not to worry about it.

About six months later they sent him a Volvo station wagon free of charge as a "thank you". They put him on the payroll as the Public Affairs person in the entertaining of the various dignitaries that came through San Francisco. At least, that's what he said.

Andy hired Forrest North, Cally's husband. Cally's name was originally Garrison. Ken had inherited Cally's father's insurance business. Garrison had a big insurance business. He represented all the people in North Beach. This included the Star Olive Oil people. He was sort of a character. He used to drive a Model T Ford, not a Model A, but a T. It was unique at that time. Cally was embarrassed when he drove her to school.

I guess it was a way to show people that he wasn't a rich man yet he lived in a beautiful house across the street from the Palace of Fine Arts on Baker Street.

When he passed away, Cally's husband was working in the business and sort of took it over. He figured there was no money in insurance. He decided to go into life insurance with mutual funds. He'd get different people like entertainers and doctors who were paying $20,000 for a million dollars' worth of life insurance. He'd give term insurance for maybe $5,000 and put the other $15,000 in mutual funds. It was a heck of a good concept, but he got greedy. Then he merged with another person who was a crook and took him down.

When that happened, Cally divorced him and the next thing he did was he was in the Veteran's nut factory. He'd been there for a year or so and Andy heard about it. He gave him a job as a gofer. He was doing a heck of a good job. So Andy said, "Want to be a salesman?"

He worked as a salesman, and was coming back. Andy had some rules. The thing about Andy is that they are very simple rules, but if you break them, you're gone. One of his rules was that you don't sell a group of vehicles, a fleet. So Forrest was working like the devil and he sold a fleet of $2 million worth of cars. He told Andy, thinking Andy would love it. Andy said, "Good-bye, Forrest."

Andy had a unique thing with the salesmen. He had four salesmen and they pooled their commissions. He wanted them to make $60,000 a year or he didn't think they were worth anything. So three of them were able to fire a fourth who wasn't able to carry his weight. So Andy had no trouble getting these salesmen because they got on each other to make sure they made that amount of money and more.

Bob Salles had a Triumph automobile and my daughter, Suzie, was going to go to college and she didn't have a car. Bob said he'd sell her the car. Promptly after that, the rear end went out. There was a maritime strike and no parts were being delivered. Andy had his boat and he took his mechanic and we went off to this Russian ship anchored in the bay. He gave the Russian guy some money, $20 or something. They found the crate where the rear end was, took it, brought it down to this boat, took it to his place of business and put the rear end back in Suzie's car in time to leave for school. There was nothing he couldn't do if you challenged him.

Just before this maritime strike, we had lunch together and I told Andy that there was going to be a strike that would shut down San Francisco, Portland and Los Angeles. He said, "I'll see you later," and he took off.

Next thing I knew, he had flown to Sweden and there was a ship that left with auto parts, so he said he'd buy a million dollars worth of parts. So they sent them to San Francisco by rail from Texas, or wherever it docked. He charged his own clients the regular price and just doubled it on anybody else wanting parts. This is how he made a lot of money.

He also had a deal with San Quentin to take paroled prisoners and give them a job so they could get back in society. He applied the same rules: if they didn't do what they were supposed to do, back to San Quentin they went. That's just the way he operated.

He bought a piece of property of 66,000 square feet down near Market Street. He got it for a reasonable price of $55,000. Today it's worth $7 million. He moved his operation down there and he would repair cars and take care of the tuning and the rest of the things that were required. He had a fellow, a big black gentleman, who lived down there. He lived up in the top. It was an old iron smelting place, and it had three stories up there where cranes could go back and forth. There was an office and a place to live. This fellow was an ex-convict. He slept there and was sort of a nightwatchman.

One night he went out for coffee, and when he came back he noticed a typewriter or something was missing. It just felt wrong. The next night he pretended to go out and then came back very quietly. He found a guy who was trying to steal some things from the office. He went after him and the guy jumped through the skylight and landed on the floor. He ended up dying. His relatives sued Andy because he was chased and he lost his way and panicked and the watchman scared him when he jumped through the skylight and was killed. They sued for $5 million. I don't think they collected, but how screwy are our laws?

The other Volvo dealers got upset at Andy because he didn't go any place and he didn't take vacations. He didn't spend the money that Volvo allotted them. Volvo gave him a credit card and said he could spend anything up to a certain amount. Andy went to what he thought was the best travel agent and gave him $500 and said, "I want to take a trip to Denmark and I want to go to Tivoli Gardens. Then I want to go to Paris and do some shopping and then I want to go to the Greek islands and I'm bringing my fiancée. I want the finest accommodations on the boat, and I want the Concorde to fly me to Denmark."

Andy gave the agent $500, and paid for everything first class. They got to Denmark and the Tivoli Gardens were closed, so they were disappointed. They went to Paris and arrived on Sunday, when everything in Paris was closed. Then they went to the Greek islands and went to Athens. Something was wrong with the ship they were supposed to go on, and they put them on this rusty old tub with bunk beds. Andy was fit to be tied. When he came back, he ended up suing this outfit for $100,000. Our son, Jimmy, handled the case and ended up collecting about $10,000. After the court costs and attorney fees, he didn't end up with anything. What got my son nuts was Andy's third wife, Eileen. She said, "Well, Andy, we had a good time. The real reason you are suing is because you're mad because you wanted to get tickets to *Phantom of the Opera* and he couldn't get them for you." Andy said, "Yeah, I guess you're right." So my son, who was negotiating the settlement, almost died when he heard that.

Years before, Andy thought he had settled with his first wife. He paid his attorney $50,000 to guarantee that the settlement he made of $2,000 or $3,000 a month, plus a new car every two years, plus 5% increase in inflation, plus vacations, etc. When he became successful, she said, "Oh, boy, I'm going to break this up." So they went to court for about six weeks.

Bob Stallings had made a deal that we would go to Mulaje, a tiny community in Baja California. I'd never been there, and Bob Stallings had put it together with a couple of friends of his. There was a pilot, Mr. Kelly; he worked for Emerson Murphy, who owned a plane and who had a restaurant in San Mateo. We were all ready to go to Mulaje and we were waiting for Andy and these other people. We all went into court around four o'clock and finally the judge came out and ruled against Andy. Andy lost about a million dollars. So off we went to Mulaje, and of course, Andy was sort of shattered.

It was a small town. When we flew in we were trying to get into the airport, but the controller at the airport was the bartender at the old motel where we were to stay. He was in the bathroom or something, so we had to circle a few times before he told us the wind conditions and to come in.

We got down there and had a few drinks in celebration and had dinner. Andy hired an orchestra. We were in the bar just talking. Andy can't read or write, but he just seems to know what is going on in a room, even though he had a few drinks. This guy came up to me. He was about 6' 1" and he was a prizefighter. He grabbed me by the neck and said, "You called me a pachuco!" – or something.

I said, "I don't even know what that means."

He wasn't going to take that, and I think he was going to practically murder me.

Andy spotted this and came over and grabbed his arm and said, "I'm afraid, will you protect me?" This guy looked like he was mesmerized by a snake charmer, and put an arm around Andy and he said, "Sure, I'll protect you." And Andy took him to the bar. Andy can fake drinking better than anybody you've ever seen. Pretty soon this guy fell of the chair. Absolutely amazing.

Next day they said, "Well, Jim, you brought your snorkel and your fins. Let's go down and take a peek and you can see if you can see something."

So I went down and dove in the estuary. It's sort of a combination of fresh and salt water. It's one of the few places in Baja where there's any fresh water above ground, from springs. I couldn't see anything, so we all went deep-sea fishing.

We hopped on a fishing boat and we went out and it was fantastic. We caught dorados, which are mahi-mahis, and we caught rooster fish and sierras. Everybody caught some fish. We came back to the hotel and the cook cooked them for us. The night before we had been soaked $125 for drinks, but no one had signed anything. Andy had a few drinks and we were playing ping-pong. He could hardly see straight, and he challenged this guy to a game at $100 a game. This was a real nice guy. I tried to talk Andy out of it, but he insisted and this guy beat him and won $100. So Andy said, "If you won $100, you have to be a sport and pay for the band and all the drinks tonight." So this guy probably ended up paying $150, and we had a free night, that night.

The next day we took a boat ride up the estuary and we were looking for these red snapper, real red snapper, not cod. I looked over and, my goodness, there were all these Portuguese men-of-war. They were a hundred to two hundred times bigger than any I'd ever seen. There were hundreds of them. If I had taken a swim in there, I would have been a dead duck. My instructor in scuba-diving and skin diving had told me never to go into a strange place where you can't see the water. Boy, that was good advice. I ended up catching more fish and one giant fish, about twenty pounds, which was the biggest red snapper that was caught throughout the area. So that was quite a time.

Bob Stallings thought that was a real good excursion, so he decided that he'd have another down to a place called Habre Ojos, which means "open eyes". In this particular case we had three planeloads. We had seven in our group, seven in Ferrari's group, and seven in Shakey Johnson's group. We couldn't believe it, but we landed on the beach. Habre Ojos is not on the inside of the Sea of Cortez, but on the ocean side. We landed on the beach and we were greeted by the mayor of Habre Ojos and there was nothing there except tents. The tents were put up and financed by a *Chronicle* sports reporter. He financed the deal with the mayor of Habre Ojos. There was nothing to see, no house, no nothing, but these tents. They had a primitive outhouse and it was terrible. They had a bucket on top, so if somebody threw some water on the top of it you could clean up. That was our shower.

So, our three planes landed, and they had gathered oysters and some small buttered clams, like Washington clams. They had fish that was barbecued, and all this was just hors d'oeuvres. We had a beautiful roast beef dinner and it was unbelievable. The next morning we woke up about 4 A.M. They had five or six young ladies and men, boatmen, who went back to town at night and returned early in the morning to start a fire and cook breakfast of *huevos rancheros*, eggs, ham, or whatever you wanted. In the morning we could go fishing and catch all kinds of fish. Around noon, the winds came up and absolutely blew you away. We decided to take a nap, so we slept from around one to four o'clock. We'd stay in or some of the guys would play poker.

After one day of this, Shakey Johnson said, "This is nuts," and he and Ferrari took off in his plane. Here we were, with Andy and Bob Stallings and Bob Leavy and a couple of other guys. I forget what their names were. We had the whole camp to ourselves and all kinds of food. They had abalone, lobster, everything. I said I'd like to go clamming and the mayor said to me, "OK, come with us."

We went out to the beach, and I started to just prance in, but the mayor stopped me and said, "Oh, no, you slide in because we have stingrays here. If you put your foot on one, it's like a two-quart tequila, because there's no medicine around here to dull the pain. Even that won't do it." He said to roll your heels around like you are doing the hula or something and when you feel a rock reach down, and there's this beautiful Pismo calm.

So I was in there about half an hour and I had a hundred pounds of Pismo clams. We were just taking them to the beach when we saw a huge tuna boat coming. It was a Boston Whaler and we were watching it. A man jumped off into the water as they were beaching the boat, and wham! He was hit by one of those stingrays. They threw him back into the Boston Whaler and took him back to the tuna boat. Then another boat came and we gave them some clams and all kinds of stuff. They came back and brought us about fifty pounds of swordfish.

San Bruno City Council

Someone suggested that I run for City Council because a race was coming up. I thought that sounded a little exciting. I wanted to get involved and I wanted to learn how to speak. I won't speak unless I'm forced to. This was the most difficult part of my life, because I almost threw up every time I had to do that. I was a terrible speaker, and to this day, I'm not very good; but it doesn't bother me like it did then. I ran for City Councilman and I was elected. Another person, Clay Fisher, was elected with me. He had some good advice. He said, "Don't ever promise to do anything for anybody, but if you ever do, keep your promise. If you do have to change your mind, you have to go back to that person and tell them you are not going to vote in their favor."

The old guard was William Mauer and John Murphy. Mauer had been on the council for about twenty-five years and Murphy had been there about sixteen years. Mauer was the Police Commissioner and Murphy was the Water Commissioner. At that time, Don Risso, Bill McGuffin, and Claude Fourie were the active people in government. Claude Fourie was mayor. He tried to compromise with the old guard and the new guard, trying to get some order out of this chaos. It was automatic that if one side voted for something, the other voted against it. As a result, nothing was accomplished.

They had just passed a city manager form of government. The only problem was that they really didn't *want* a city manager form of government. They wanted a manager with a commission form of government, keeping the Police, Fire, and Water commissions.

They appointed a city manager named Matt Slankert. He was an aggressive gentleman. We then started to address some of the issues that were bothering some of the new arrivals in San Bruno. The War Memorial Community Center (called the Recreation Center) was not finished. There was wiring and everything hanging out, and it looked terrible. Then there was a need for a new City Hall. We had a dinky place on El Camino Real next to a hat store. We needed library services and the most pressing need was a facility for the Police and Fire Department, and a jail.

We were addressing these problems when a bombshell hit. Willie Mauer found out that Matt Slankert had falsified his application. He had said he had been City Manager or an Assistant City Manager when the highest level he had attained before was as a water meter reader for some city. Matt claimed that Mayor Fourie knew it.

Anyway, Slankert was fired, with no objection. Then Matt Slankert called the heads of Swift Company, where Murphy worked, and told them Fourie was a crook, and no good, etc. So the heads of Swift called Fourie and told him to resign as mayor or be fired. Fourie promptly resigned. Actually, he was nowhere near a crook. He was one of the nicest persons you'd ever want to meet.

City Council of San Bruno, 1952

Mayor of San Bruno

So there we were, without a mayor. It was customary in those days to have an "executive session" in the back room. I suggested to Mr. Mauer that, having been on the board for twenty-five years, and never having served as mayor, he should be nominated. He said, "Oh, no. You're not going to trap me like that."

Mr. Mauer was an interesting person. He wore a cape, derby hat, celluloid collar and tie. He was a very, very, unusual man. So I suggested to Mr. Murphy, being the next senior member, that he might be mayor. "Oh, no, I don't want to be mayor." Mr. Fisher also declined. They said, "That leaves you." So that's how I became mayor of the City of San Bruno.

No one paid attention when Fisher and I were elected, because everyone knew the Mauer and Murphy ran things anyway. The mayor actually had very little power; he was just the same as any other city councilman. I found, however, that the mayor does have one little bit of power. He has the power of selecting the Commissioners. My thinking was that Mauer had been Police Commissioner for twenty-five years, and a real good friend of Artichoke Joe and the owner of the other card room in town. I said that Mr. Mauer, instead of being Police Commissioner, should be Planning Commissioner. He refused to take it. I named Mr. Murphy, instead of Water Commissioner, to the Recreation Commission. He refused. I told the remaining two members beside myself, that we would just have to double up on the job. I didn't realize the significance at the time, but the headlines the next day read:

FITZGERALD TAKES OVER – MAUER/MURPHY ARE OUT!

In politics, it's not the way it really is, it's the way it seems to be.

As a result of this perception, psychologically, but not actually, things changed. We levied a three-cent tax and completed the War

Memorial Building (the Recreation Building in the park). We then had an election and we covered the Belle Aire Canal.

There was a City Engineer who looked like a little tiny Santa Claus. Everybody loved him. He had a smile all the time. He came in, took over as City Manager, and everything seemed to be working very smoothly. I said, "Mr. White, how come everything is so calm and all these big problems seem to disappear."

He said, "Mr. Fitzgerald, I'll tell you. What's your question, exactly?"

I said, "Well, suppose we go ahead and we say we want you to check all the streets and re-pave all the streets in a certain district. What would you do with that?"

"Oh," he said, "I'd put that in one file."

I said, "Well, say we're going to put up $5,000 to pave a particular street."

"Oh," he said, "that goes into another file. That's the one that I take care of. I don't pay any attention to the other one until the money's there."

I said, "What do you do with the big problems?"

He said, "Mr. Fitzgerald, I just refer them to the wisdom of the City Council and the mayor, and they solve all the big problems, so I have no worries at all."

This was a lesson. That's the way he worked, and he was pretty smart. He did what the council wanted and ran the city.

I used to meet with the mayors of Millbrae and South San Francisco. We'd have lunch and talk. The other two mayors were Earl Wilmes of the Millbrae El Rancho Hotel, and Guido Rozzi of South San Francisco. One day we decided, we all had these same budget problems and the smartest thing to do would really be to merge the three cities.

At that time, there were only about 20,000 people in each city. If you had a police department and you maybe had ten men in the police department, you could only have two cars. People think you run a police car with one man. Well, he works forty hours a week. Every day had twenty-four hours, so one man works eight and the second man works eight and the third man works eight. That takes care of five days. Then the fourth man works on Saturday eight hours, the fifth man works eight hours and the sixth man works the third shift. Then you have vacations and holidays. So you have at least five men to a police car. If you have a detective and a chief and twelve policemen, you have two automobiles.

The same thing applies to the fire department. They're on twenty-four hours and sleep on the job. If they were on two days, that's forty-eight hours. Theoretically, they could have the next five days off. But there are some catches. They can't have the days all together. Most of the firemen had other jobs contracting, etc., on their days off.

I had an insurance client once who was a Battalion Chief in San Francisco, Ed O'Dowd. He had a driver and he'd buy a piece of property that was old and he would fix it up. His chauffeur told me later, "We'd drive by Cleveland Wrecking and he'd say, 'Stop, we've got to pick up some used toilets and drop them off at my property.'" He ended up with about $4 or $5 million worth of property in the Marina District in San Francisco.

One time the City of San Francisco gave me an invitation because I was a good friend with the then mayor, George Christopher. It was a sister city thing from San Francisco to Osaka, Japan. We were to go to Japan. My friend, Bob Salles, said, "Gee, that sounds like a good deal. Could you get me in on it?" I phoned and they had a vacancy in the party and he came with us.

We had the Takahashis and Cyril Magnin and all the wheels of San Francisco. There were a lot of Asian people, and some were going back to meet their relatives and were real worried because they had forgotten how to speak Japanese fluently. We got on the plane; it was a charter Japanese Airline plane. Well, everyone started partying and they were drinking everything that was on the plane. We landed in Japan and they cleared the streets and took us to a hotel and we were treated like kings. The next day we went out to the Exposition and they had some ceremonies and they had geisha girls and it was really something. Every night they had cocktail parties and they had so much food at the parties that you really didn't have to go out to eat. The only thing that upset my wife was that they said they had whiskey, but the whiskey they had was Scotch, not bourbon.

The mayor of Osaka invited us to go to a luncheon at the Osaka Palace. It was beautiful, and we had a most fantastic time. We had lobster, we had prawn, we had all kinds of things. It was a very elaborate meal. We took a picture, the mayor and me, because, I guess I was a mayor, too. I was talking to the mayor's wife and I said, "Gee, these geisha girls are really beautiful. How much do those costumes cost?"

She said, "Oh, the costumes are worth five or ten thousand dollars. I never saw a geisha girl before. This is the first time that they've come out in public."

I told her that I didn't realize that. She said, "My husband knows all of them, but I've never seen them before."

My wife and I were going out to a place to eat. I had mentioned the place to the mayor's wife and she had said it was a gyp joint and we shouldn't go there. We tried to get in anyhow, but we couldn't. The doorman was real nice and he sent us down the street about three blocks to a little Japanese inn. It was a fabulous meal and it was real Japan.

Next, we went to Taiwan, a beautiful and interesting place, and then to Hong Kong. In Hong Kong, they said to go to Han Sin Tailors. They said it was a really legitimate place and they wouldn't gyp you. If you didn't like the suit, you wouldn't have to pay for it. We went there with Bob Salles, and he got measured for a suit. My wife was yelling at me to get a suit, but I didn't want a suit. Finally, I gave in and agreed to get a sport's coat. You pick out the material you want and they make it for you in three or four days. You have to go in for a couple of fittings. Bob got a sport's coat and a suit.

The next day the girls wanted to go to Mikimoto's to get some pearls. While we were waiting, Bob bought some silk shirts. He paid about $5 each for them, and he thought it was a good buy. We were walking along and a man from India came up and asked if we had bought any silk shirts. Bob said, "Yes, I got them for $5." The man said, "Ouch, you got stuck. I can give you these shirts for $2."

Bob said, "They must be different."

We went in and they were the same shirts. So the guy says, "What about selling you a suit?"

Bob said, "We went to Han Sin's."

The guy says, "They're bandits. I bet they charged you $125."

Bob said, "Yes."

"Well," the guy said, "we'll charge $75 and you can pick out any kind of material. How much did you pay for the sport's coat?"

Bob said, "$75."

The man said, "We can do it for $50."

Bob got fitted for it. When we were ready to leave Hong Kong, Bob's wife, Claire, told me to go with Bob to pick the clothes up, because he wasn't going to buy the suit. I said that he'd already paid Han Sin's. She told me that he hadn't paid Han Sin, but he had paid the other place. We went to Han Sin's, and he tried on the suit and sport coat and paid for them in cash. We went to the other place, and I knew there would be trouble. He tried on the suit and it was all cockeyed. One shoulder was up and one was down. It was really a terrible suit. They said, "I'm sorry, we can't do anything."

So I started screaming and I told them we would go to the British Consulate and tell them that this was a gyp joint. The owner came in and I told him we want our money back.

He said, "No, the man came in and got a fitting. He wasn't properly attired when he got his fitting. He came in with a sports shirt and he wasn't wearing a dress shirt and tie." Then he said, "We're not going to give you the money back."

So that's the way it was. But we didn't get killed and it was a fantastic trip.

Civic Buildings

Even though it was lousy water, we were making so much money in the San Bruno Water Department that we were able to build the City Hall for a little over $300,000. Today the replacement of it would run to about $4,500,000. The main library was about $150,000, and the children's library was $9,000. The two-stage Community Center ran about $350,000. All these things were paid for in a three-year period. We built a swimming pool which ran about $90,000. The only thing we had to go to a bond issue for was the Fire Department and some trucks and water mains. The bond issue did not pass the first time, but it passed on the second try.

When we decided the library needed some improvement, it was on the site of the present Bank of America building. We had some space on the Civic Center property which couldn't be used for anything else, where the City Hall is now. It wouldn't cost us a cent for land cost to put the library there. Well, we didn't have any money to do it, but we could sell the old library site. It was voted down three to two by the City Council. We went to an election, because you need a four-fifths vote to sell a piece of city property. It passed.

Modesta Peterson was in charge. She phoned every person individually who was listed in the telephone book who lived in San Bruno. She was a fantastic woman, completely dedicated to San Bruno. We put the property up for sale, and the Bank of America paid us around $125,000. We used that to build the library.

It was interesting working with people, which I was used to in the real estate and insurance business. Even though I was still only thirty years old, there was a problem that came up and I needed to talk with Andy Oddstad about it. Andy was a real fine gentleman from Oddstad Homes. I told him, "You are building all these houses up here, but you're really not contributing. We've already built the City Hall, library, and all you new young people are going to get use of these facilities. I think you should pay $100 per lot so that we could build a swimming pool and children's library with the money."

He thought that was a fair request, after I talked to him several times. Legally, we could not force it. It would have to be done voluntarily. We passed an ordinance or memorandum that this is what we would require from each developer. All of a sudden, the building contractors' association came down on us like a ton of bricks. They said we couldn't do it, as it was against the law. Andy Oddstad was good enough to talk to them, and we had meetings to explain exactly what we would do with the money. We were not going to use it for maintenance or repairs. We were going to use it to expand facilities for the new people who were coming in.

Even though it wasn't legal, they went ahead and contributed voluntarily their $100, and that's how we were able to put in the swimming pool and the children's library.

Linda Mar

Andy Oddstadt was a nephew of Stoneson of Stoneson Development, the company that built Stownstown Shopping Center. They didn't pay any attention to him there. He was Icelandic, and he just started hammering on wallboards and doing carpentry work and went into business for himself and became very successful. He was building in Linda Mar, now in the city of Pacifica, and came to a point where he was stopped. They didn't have enough water. He was concerned that if there was a fire, there wouldn't be any water at all.

He came over the hill to San Bruno to talk to me. He said he'd build a line from Linda Mar over to San Bruno, and put up a five-million gallon water tank that San Bruno could use, too. It would be used for storage for water to go down to Linda Mar. He'd take care of the whole works to build it and we wouldn't have to worry about it. He couldn't buy water from the City of San Francisco's Hetch Hetchy system, because Linda Mar was privately owned. We, as a city, could buy water from Hetch Hetchy and resell it to him. I told him we would have to charge a 15% brokerage commission on this, and he said this was fine. I have pictures of the construction of this fabulous water line. It went over the hill from San Bruno connecting to the Hetch Hetchy water system. There is this big tank and then the water continues down the hill to Linda Mar.

The water department down on the coast was very, very upset about this, yet they couldn't provide the service. They came and had a meeting with the San Bruno City Council and everybody was screaming at everybody. What happened was the engineer for the North Coast Water District dropped dead at the council meeting. That was a *scary* night! Our City Engineer, Dan Russell, didn't look good, like he was going to drop dead, but he did live for a while after that. Finally, we did supply the water for Linda Mar. Andy said that as long as we were providing the water service, why didn't we annex the property into San Bruno? The City Council okayed that. Oddstadt was going to build a road over the top of the hill connecting Linda Mar to San Bruno.

However, the San Bruno people got a resolution together and an election killed the annexation. Some people call me the "Bastard Father of Pacifica" because soon after this the people from all the little areas on the coast got together and decided to form a city of Pacifica so that Jim Fitzgerald wouldn't go over there and grab them and eat them up! So that's how Pacifica got started.

The sad thing is that I hear from a friend in the Water Department of San Bruno that they don't use this water line any more. The pipes are full of holes. That's too bad, because San Bruno could continue to make money from that program.

Parks and Trees

During this time, there was a lot of rain. There were mudslides
and all kinds of things. They were starting to develop Crestmoor
Park and it became flooded. There was mud in the downtown
San Mateo Avenue area. The mud was six inches deep because of
the flooding caused by the grading of the land in Crestmoor Park.
At that time, I sat down with the developers, Martin Wonderlich,
especially. I told them we couldn't have this happening. They had
to clean up the mess and they wouldn't be able to build anything
until they developed a system. They needed a dam, some piping,
and so forth, which would allow a gradual run-off of the water in
case of another flood. I asked for some tree belts, because they had
knocked down most of the trees in the area. The staff of the City
of San Bruno did not want us to take the tree belts because there
were no funds for them. We insisted. We bought little pine
seedlings for about five cents each from the Department of
Forestry. I know I planted about a hundred, and I know people
who planted thousands of those trees. That was over forty years
ago, and now the trees are getting old and need a lot of attention.
One of the beauties of San Bruno is if you stand back and look, as
I have, you'll see thousands and thousands of trees. You realize
the people who were in Crestmoor Park and Rollingwood took
the time and effort to plant those trees. To me, that was an
outstanding job of cooperation.

I also asked for twenty acres of land, which the builders agreed
to. That land is the seven acres adjoining San Bruno Park and five
acres of the Buckeye Grove. I left the Council before the rest of
the acreage was decided on.

There's a picture in my scrapbook of Mr. Wonderlich and
myself taking the barriers off San Bruno Avenue. Mr.
Wonderlich, of the Consolidated Land Company, was the one
who agreed to pay for half or more of the cost of San Bruno
Avenue, so that we would have a good connecting street between

freeways 280 and 101. He was a great man. He owned fifty per cent of the Consolidated Land Company, and he was easy to deal with. The other partners included George W. Williams and Frank Bowwers. They were real tough businessmen. The other player was Conway and Culligan, which was sort of like the minority group. But these were a whole bunch of quarterbacks. Everybody wanted to run the organization. There was one person who quietly did so, and that was Martin Wonderlich. He owned fifty per cent.

San Francisco Airport

Another interesting thing at that time was the expansion of the San Francisco Airport. They were bringing in tons and tons of dirt from the hills down San Bruno Avenue. These big semi-trucks and trailers were playing havoc with our streets. They were going from the morning at 4 A.M. We protested to the truckers and nothing happened. Finally someone suggested I speak to the Truckers' Union head, Hank Schram. I talked to him and he said he could see we had a problem. He made arrangements to start the trucking at 7:30 or 8 A.M. That was a big improvement, but we hadn't figured out how to take care of the street repairs. It was interesting working with him, and finally we got the truck bosses to see the damage they had done. We said we wanted a couple of cents per yard of dirt hauled for the damage. They didn't want any part of this, and finally I said that we wouldn't use the money for operating our government. We offered to make a special trust fund just for repair and maintenance of the road, and they could be a trustee in the fund.

They didn't do much of anything, so we started looking for truck violations. We stopped every third truck to make sure their lights were OK, and so on. Pretty soon they agreed that they would sign a contract and put aside two cents, or whatever, for each yard of dirt they hauled through San Bruno. Legally, we could not charge them. It had to be voluntary. But it worked.

Moving On

A point came when I felt that everything I thought should be done in the City of San Bruno was done and paid for. There really wasn't much left to do. It was just maintenance, and I wouldn't be happy in the position of being a mayor or councilman in a maintenance program. It's interesting to note that to this day, only a few civic buildings have been built there since the 1950s, and these include the Senior Citizen's Building on Crystal Springs Road and the Police Building. The Firehouse and library and the pool in the park are there, and the extended acreage and City Hall. All these things were done during that time, and there's no debt in the city as far as I know. At least we didn't create any debt, except for the improvements, which were amortized many, many years ago. I had found that I really enjoyed the excitement of politics. I decided to run for the County Board of Supervisors.

My father had always believed that I had an obligation to give back to this wonderful country, the USA. Unfortunately, my father passed away before I was elected supervisor.

I ran against a gentleman named Tom Callan. Tom had come from Ireland. He was a self-made man who lived up in Colma and started out raising pigs. With the money he made with the pigs, he bought property and became an excellent purchaser of tax delinquent lots. After twenty or thirty years, he had amassed over 5,000 parcels of property. Some parcels were 2,000 acres. One of these parcels is now the Westborough area in South San Francisco. Tom Callan was a County Supervisor for many years, and I decided to run against him.

A man named Serrini, who I felt was a friend of mine before the election, never supported me. Maybe fifteen years after the election, he took me to lunch to explain why he didn't support me. He said, "Well, I want to tell you, Jim, I was a pig farmer. I was just starting out with my wife and I had an interest in this pig farm. I had a partner who put up all the money, and when we were ready to sell the pigs, we were to take out the expenses and split the profit. When that time came, he came to me and said he wanted $20,000. I didn't have $20,000, and I went to the bank and all over the place, but I couldn't get any money at all. So I went to Tom Callan and he said to go to the bank and he would sign for me. I got the $20,000 and I was able to get my share of the profit from the pigs." I realized Tom Callan was a good person, no doubt about that.

I rang 5,000 doorbells and gathered about $10,000 to $15,000. It was an interesting experience. I was ringing doorbells, and I met this gentleman who asked if I knew a certain lady who lived in Hillsborough. I said I didn't know her. He said she was the daughter of the former president of Southern Pacific, and she was a nice lady. He said he would phone and see if she was interested in supporting me. He did and phoned me and told me she would like me to come up and see her. I went up and saw her and her husband. They lived in a lovely home, and after we'd talked she said she would like to help me. She asked for the name of my campaign manager and public relations person. I gave her the name of my campaign manager. She sent out 35,000 letters on my behalf to be elected. She never phoned me again or asked me for any favors when I became a member of the Board of Supervisors.

Another interesting thing: I received a check from Lurline Roth, whose grandfather was the founder of the Matson shipping line. One of the ships was named *Lurline* after her. Many of these well-known people felt that they had to give back to the community that they had gotten a lot from.

Another gentleman, John Romano, was also running for supervisor. After a long and trying campaign, I won by 45,000 votes to 44,000 and John Romano got about 5,000 votes. Neither Tom Callan nor I had the authority, so we had to have a run-off election in November.

Mr. Callan decided to put some of his own money into it, and really run a campaign. It was tough and after another four or five months, the election came in. I was at my house, and my former partner, Al Hansen, was there with Jean and some friends. At 2 A.M., I was about 2,000 votes behind, and it looked like it was all over. I went to sleep and woke up about 7:00 and found that I was gaining. I was about 500 votes behind. My partner used some algebra and said that by 8:30, I would be ahead. Sure enough, whether I was lucky or not, I went ahead. I was ahead by 500 votes when the regular votes were counted. But there were 5,000 absentee votes that still had to be counted. Usually, the incumbent gets most of the absentee votes.

I was so tired that we went to Carmel. We were both so bushed we accidentally left all our luggage at home. We didn't even have a toothbrush. I was so exhausted, I didn't care. They sent our luggage down by Greyhound bus.

It was five or six days later that they finished counting the absentee ballots, and I won by about 500 votes and became County Supervisor, representing the north end of the County. In those days we were elected at large, meaning by the whole county instead of just your area.

All the other four supervisors had backed Tom Callan. I thought it was going to be a little difficult, and they wouldn't be nice to me and so forth. I was completely wrong. When I came on the Board, they all acknowledged that they had supported the other man and he was their friend; but now that I was on the Board of Supervisors, that was past, and we were all going to work together.

I have to say that I have never met a finer group of men in my whole life. Alvin Hatch at that time was eighty-five. He stayed on the board until he was ninety, and he was sharp as a tack. He was a former lumberman. There was Ed McDonald, and he was a former druggist. He was also a sharp guy. His health wasn't the best. He was seventy-six years old. He was the only Democrat, but you couldn't tell the Democrats from the Republicans, because the Board was non-partisan. We voted what was best for the County.

Then there was Louie Chess. He was a dynamo. He ran the Southern Pacific Western Division trains. I would say he knew seventy-five per cent of the people in San Mateo County. They all knew Louie Chess. His real name was Chezio Luigi Chesola. Then there was Bill Werder, who had been a straight A student at

Stanford. He was a track star who just missed the Olympics by the skin of his teeth, or, I should say, by six inches in the broad jump. His biggest problem was that he liked girls. He was brilliant, but he was a playboy. He made a lot of money, but he switched wives with one of his best friends and it ended in divorce. It was a shame, because the guy was so smart, he could have been President of the United States – if he hadn't been distracted. Or he could at least have been a Senator. He was so well educated and he could "charm the birds out of the trees". He was the young guy until I got there. He was about fifty-five then, and I was about forty.

County Board of Supervisors

The first thing I got involved in was the project to build a courthouse in either Daly City or South San Francisco. On investigating the two sites, I determined we should put the courtrooms in South San Francisco. We had one judge then who was holding court in Daly City, so he wanted it to be Daly City. Then he decided he wanted to design a courtroom. The estimated cost of his courtroom was $400,000. I checked and found that we had just built three courtrooms in the City of San Mateo that had cost $250,000.

I figured it would be smart to use those same architectural plans in South San Francisco. We could build three courtrooms cheaper than his design for one. You can't believe the commotion this caused, and Judge Becker wouldn't sign the plans. The other members of the Board backed me, and we finally succeeded in building the courtrooms. Just to satisfy the judge, he had to screw around with the plans and put the judge's chair way up in the air, so he could hardly see anything. Completing the courtrooms was my first success.

We had one room there, and we all sat around a big table. We met every Tuesday, and before we would go on with the meeting, we would talk about anything that was concerning any of us. "What do you think about this or that?" We would get everyone's opinions, but nobody would say which way they were going to vote. If you listened, you could figure it out, but no one committed themselves. I think it was Clay Fisher who said, "You never promise your vote to anyone." They would ask for your vote, and you just say, "At the right time, all things being equal, you are going to be given every consideration." That is the way it should be.

We had one secretary for the five Board members. We usually met in the morning and adjourned for lunch. In the afternoon, sometimes the meetings would go until 5:00. There were a lot of things to do. The agenda consisted of anything anyone wanted to write to us about. Sometimes there were forty or fifty items. They would call and talk to June, the Clerk of the Board, and she'd tell them when we would probably get to an item. At that time the person would get up and say, "You donkeys, you know you did this wrong, and you should have done that."

We'd answer as best we could. It was a way people could vent their problems and talk directly to all of the supervisors. My phone number was in the telephone book. People could pick up the phone and call me at home. There was no one in between me and the public. I'm sure the other supervisors had their numbers listed, too.

Every other Thursday we would go on field trips. At this time we represented all the unincorporated area. We did not represent the cities. Now the supervisors represent what is left of the unincorporated areas. Back then, it included Half Moon Bay, Brisbane, Foster City, East Palo Alto, Portola Valley, and Woodside. We acted like a city council for those cities. Mostly, we dealt with zoning problems. We'd hop in the car on Thursday and go see the site. We would be followed by the planning director and his staff. We'd look and listen to the problem. When the matter came up before the Board, we'd know exactly what we were talking about. We'd go to Pescadero or Half Moon Bay. We had problems all over the place.

We were also the Tax Appeal Board. One year we had over 600 tax appeal decisions to make. It was a quasi-judicial procedure. You bring in the matter and you say you disagree with the assessor, and the assessor explains why he assessed some property as he did, show comparables, and so forth. We listened to all of this. Some cases took an hour. We were in session every day for several months listening to these tax appeal problems.

At Board Meetings, we would go in and go through the agenda. Bob Stallings was the County Manager. He was a genius. He could have been a Donald Trump. But again, he sort of liked the booze and the ladies. Otherwise, he would have been a super person as a City Manager say, in New York or San Francisco or wherever. I think we were paying him $60,000 at the time, which was a pretty good salary. He was worth it. He would bring up the agenda items and make his recommendations. Normally speaking, he sort of knew what would go over and what wouldn't. If we had any concerns about anything, he would lay it over and we could talk about our problems with it, and so forth.

County Disaster Office

When you're the freshman member, the Board of Supervisors gives you the dirty jobs. They rewarded me by making me the Civil Defense and Disaster Chief.

There was nothing much to do as the Disaster Chief because there hadn't been any disasters. There was no Civil Defense program. We were just sort of looking into this when the Russians, during the Cold War, were bringing their ships into Cuba. The big showdown between Kennedy and Khrushchev had not been resolved, and people were starting to panic and think there was going to be a nuclear war. They started calling me as Civil Defense Chief and asking if they should get underneath their cars or what they should do. The most asked question was, "Where are the County shelters?"

When I told them we didn't have any and we really didn't know how to protect ourselves against a nuclear warfare, I was chastised. They couldn't imagine how there were no civil defense shelters. It was terrible. That was one of the worst times in my life. I had nightmares imagining we had a nuclear disaster and we had no way to combat it. Fortunately, it never happened. We then realized we needed to get some form of Disaster Program, even though a nuclear disaster wasn't anything we could handle, we should at least be able to take care of a natural disaster.

I was sitting quietly eating my dinner one night when the Sheriff called. It was raining like the dickens that night. The Sheriff was up on the Half Moon Bay Highway, Highway 92, calling from a phone booth. He wanted me to get the National Guard out. When I asked him what for, he said that Pacifica was under water. The creek had overflowed, and there was about eight feet of water on the highway. Young kids with surfboards were vandalizing and robbing various properties, smashing the windows and going into houses with their surfboards. So I called the Governor's office and got some aid. The National Guard was called out and the looting was stopped. The next morning I got up at about six and went over there. I could see there was about three or four feet of mud on Highway 1 and it was a big mess. Cars had slid out of control. Everybody was screaming, "You've got to do something."

So I called out the County Engineering Department and promptly cleaned everything up, to the tune of about $50,000. I think it was Sunday. The Board met on Tuesdays. When I got to the meeting, I explained what I had done, and that the initial cost was $50,000. The District Attorney said, "I'm sorry, Mr. Fitzgerald, but you had no authority to do that. You can't go out spending public funds without a resolution of the Board of Supervisors, and there had been no resolution."

So I looked at my pals of the Board and said, "You guys gave me this job. I did what was necessary." Everybody, including the District Attorney, agreed. The County Engineer said that it had to be done or somebody was going to be killed, sliding around in the mud like that. Finally the members of the Board, the Chairman, said, "Well, when we appointed you, we all agreed and we told you that we'd back you up one hundred per cent, and that if there was any disaster or emergency that we would make the necessary expenditures."

So they passed a resolution for expenditures of $50,000 and took me off the hook. Otherwise, I'd have been broke! At that time I'd have been more than broke. I decided that if they wanted me to continue on the job they would have to put $50,000 in a revolving fund so that I, or anyone in my position, could access it if anything like this came up in the future. Otherwise, we'd be murdered by the public if we didn't take care of something like this. It wouldn't happen that often. We organized the Civil Defense and Disaster Committee, with one representative from each of the mayors and the Board of Supervisors. As I thought about what had happened, it crossed my mind that the City of Pacifica should put up some of the money. When we requested it, they did.

Another evening I received a call at 8 P.M. that we had a house that was going to be demolished by a landslide in the unincorporated area near Daly City. My wife and I hopped in the car and went sailing up there and told the engineer to meet us. We got there and the mud was pressing against the bedroom of the house with such strength that the mud was pushing through the slats in the wood siding. With the engineer, I decided to tell him to bring out the crew and attempt to shovel away the dirt that was coming down the hillside and moving against the house. They called out the Engineering Department and the Road Department, but unfortunately they couldn't get any equipment back there because the houses were so close together. It all had to be done by shovel and wheelbarrow, and then haul the dirt away by truck. We left at about 10 P.M. to go home and get some sleep.

The next morning I want back and there were about a hundred residents out there in the street. The road crew had worked all night and they were tired and had to go home, but there were no substitutes. The people there said, "If you leave the shovels and wheelbarrows, we'll be happy to go on and move the dirt, providing the engineer and the property owner tell us what needs to be done. We asked where the owner of the property was. He wasn't there, and someone said he's probably up at the bar."

The Chief of the Broadmoor Police was there and he said he knew where the owner was. So he went and brought him down. Everyone was standing there wanting to help. We were going to leave an engineer to advise him of what to do, and if he made the decision, these people would remove the dirt. The property owner said, "I'm not going to do that. You people have assumed this responsibility, and I'm going to let you complete the job. I'm not going to help you at all."

We asked, "What are you talking about?"

He said, "My attorney, Mr. Haggerty told me to do this."

Everybody packed up and went home. He lost his house and sued the County and lost. It was a sad case, because all he had to do was to do what the engineer told him and his house could have been saved.

Speaking of Mr. Haggerty, I had another problem when I was on the Board of Supervisors. I wasn't doing any real estate work, but I had sold this lady a pair of flats in the Marina. She had paid the highest price for them, and I had sold her some income property in the San Carlos business area. This all took place before I was on the Board. I got a call from her one day and she asked to see me. I said I'd be happy to see her. She had an expensive home down in Atherton. She was about sixty and weighed about 250 or 300 pounds. There was a young man or about forty there. He was a swarthy, dark person. She introduced him as Nick. She said he'd been helping her with her one hundred-unit motel and various properties, doing painting and things. She said he was also a bartender. I said, "OK." Then she said she wanted to show me this nice wristwatch he gave her. I know nothing about jewelry, but it looked to me like costume jewelry with all these fake diamonds on it. I asked what she wanted to see me about. She said Nick had a house in San Francisco that he would like to sell. I told her that I wasn't in the real estate business any more.

"Well," she said, "I've been a very good customer of yours, and I wish you would help us out and see to it that this house is sold."

I told her I would see what I could do. He signed a contract and I asked a friend if he was interested in selling this house, and he said yes. After about fifty days, I called and my friend said he had a buyer and it was in the Title Company and the deal was finished. Everybody got their money, and I thought that was the quietest deal I've ever seen in real estate. A few months later I read in the paper about Dr. Brady and Dr. Brumback. They were very well known on radio, probably the only two dentists in San Francisco who advertised in those days. One of them was caught acting as a fence. He had something like $700,000 worth of jewelry. He confessed that he got the jewelry from this Nick.

I thought, Oh, my God. I'd better forget I had anything to do with him, being that I was on the Board of Supervisors. Things were quiet for about a month and then I received a call from this attorney Mr. Haggerty. He said, "We have this client named Nick, who says he knows you."

I said, "Nick who?"

He said that he had him there and he says that I handled a real estate deal for him. I said that I really didn't handle it, but a friend of mine handled it.

He said, "Well you are the one he gave the contract to."

I said, "Yeah, I guess that's right."

Haggerty asked if I had any arguments on the sale of the property.

I said, "No, I didn't really have anything to do with it. I signed the contract, gave it to another broker and he sold it. That's all I know about it. I assume he got the money and everything else."

Haggerty said, "It's a good thing you didn't get into any arguments because Nick has been on drugs and has probably killed a half dozen people. He's been in Alcatraz. Do you know where his lady friend is now?"

I told him I didn't know. Apparently she grabbed the money and he never got the money for the house. That was a crazy story, but it was true. That was Mr. Haggerty. The reason he knew me was that we used to play handball down at the Olympic Club.

I was driving down Bayshore Highway one day, when I heard on the radio that a Japanese Airlines plane had just landed in the Bay while attempting to land at the San Francisco International Airport. I headed for the Coyote Point area where they were supposed to have landed and I called out the ambulances in case of injuries. It was foggy as the dickens, but you could see these rubber boats on the water. I was there before the boats landed. They all paddled in, and fortunately no one was hurt. The plane landed in about eight feet of water and mud. The plane was severely damaged, but I don't believe we used the ambulances. It was one of those things. It was better having them available in case someone had a life-threatening problem.

It was obvious we didn't have a very good communications system. In that first case, the Sheriff had to go find a payphone to call me. That was ridiculous. I got all the mayors together and we formed a Civil Defense and Disaster Council. We all agreed to put up a microwave system to each city to be used in an emergency. Everybody put up their fair share. We had meetings and worked together just in case a disaster came. We agreed that we would utilize everybody's staff – Engineering Department, Water Works, Fire Department, Police Department. So we developed a contract on that basis. It was very good. In the meantime, the courts found out that this microwave system wasn't being used in the daytime, so they used it for sending notices about fines, traffic violations and everything over this free line instead of over the

Pacific Bell Telephone Company lines. It saved them $50 to $100 thousand a year in phone bills. I assume it's still being used for this purpose. That was a real plus, and I hope it's still working.

Later on, I felt that if we could work in this manner, why not form a congress of elected officials? In San Mateo County alone, it's hard for anybody to believe that there are over 130 taxation districts. There are twenty cities that are taxed, there are about thirty school districts, there are fire districts, there are water districts, there are all kinds of districts adding up to about 130. My thought was that we would get representatives from all the districts together to somehow unify all of the sub districts.

We had people from the heads of the school districts and the sewer districts and the fire districts and the cities and County meet. The object was to find ways that we can reduce the cost of government without hurting anybody. The first thing we discussed was that we (the cities, County, schools, etc.) all purchased common items that we needed for our facilities: things like toilet paper, soap, paper and different materials. I suggested that we choose the City of San Mateo, or the District of Menlo Park, or whoever had the best facilities and could make the best deals in purchasing to buy all the supplies so we could save money, rather than have 130 different purchasing agents buying all the items that most of us use. They worked on that. Then I suggested that one city, San Mateo or someone, do all the street work. They would contract with us and each city would pay for whatever service they needed. In that way, you don't have to have your own street department or whatever service was redundant. There definitely were certain areas where all of us could benefit.

It started off pretty well, but then the implementation became difficult and near impossible because people do not want to give up anything. That's the way it is in cities and counties, and in fact, all public agencies. They think the more they have to do the more money they will get. If they get anything cut down, they figure they're going to lose their money. In spite of it all, I thought it was a good idea and I still think so.

It came to our attention on the Board of Supervisors that we had a County Fire Department that took care of Crystal Springs watershed and the various forested areas within the County. They were not taking care of structural fires in the cities or anywhere near the cities. They were just taking care of the woods, so to speak. Checking around, I found that the State of California offered this service. I asked the State then if they would take over the wooded areas in San Mateo County. The State said sure, they did it for all the other counties, they would be glad to do it for us. This would save the County a great deal of money by eliminating the County Fire Department. But when you eliminate any jobs or departments in politics and government agencies, everything is misconstrued and all kinds of tricks are used to, you might say, "screw the works up".

This case was the first and the last time that I ever really got pressured either on the City Council or on the Board of Supervisors. When a group of firemen came in and asked me how I was going to vote on eliminating the Fire District and having the California Department of Forestry take over the work, I said I was going to vote for it. They proceeded to tell me that they were going to go out to get me and I would never be elected to a County office or city office because they had a pretty good organization and they were going to fix me up. I told them that frankly, when I looked at how much I am making (at this time it was $400 or $500 a month) they were not going to hurt me. They were going to hurt the people, I reckoned. I'd just go back to my real estate and insurance business and I'd certainly make more money than I was making in County government. This was true.

They walked out, and it's strange that I have never had any more pressure after that. Another reason I didn't have any pressure was that I was consistent. For the most part, people knew how I was going to vote. I never was pushed or anything by any political groups.

One day I asked a lobbyist who was a past mayor of Daly City how come he never dropped in to see me, but he saw the other members of the Board. He said, "Well, I want to tell you something. These people can't make up their minds on what they're going to do. So, I have to figure out some nice thing to do for them so they'll do it my way. But, I know how you're going to vote. You are either going to vote for it or against it, and whatever I do is not going to have any effect on you in any way. That's why

I don't see you. The people in politics that can't make up their minds are the people that keep me in business." I considered that a compliment.

I remember, we had these voting machines. They cost us $1,500,000 per year to lease. We didn't own them. We had to move them and buy warehouse space for them. They cost us a couple of million a year, just to have them every two years to vote. Bob Stalling, the County Manager, said, "Let me think about this." He was not just a nine to five guy. He may show up at 10 A.M. or noon sometimes, but when he had a project, he was there morning and night. He worked all hours trying to solve a problem. In this case, he did this for about a week, and then came back and said, "I think I have the solution.

"What we'll do is form a non-profit corporation. Then we'll take the money and buy the machines. We have this property out on the side of a hill. We'll build a building up the side of the hill and have driveways so that you just drive in with these heavy voting machines and slide them off at each floor. By doing that, we can save $400,000 a year."

It worked out. He had the idea and not only that; he could put the idea into effect. I guess it's still working.

Tourism

Today tourism brings in over a billion and a half of new money to San Mateo County. The occupancy tax gives the cities and county over $100 million per year. It wasn't that way around 1965. George Petroff, who was a former public relations executive at Pan American Airways, kept telling me that we needed a Tourist and Convention Bureau. He agreed to take me to Hawaii to meet the expert who ran the Hawaii Tourist Bureau, which was a fabulous success. I went and met the tourist genius. He agreed to draw up a plan for San Mateo County for $10,000 instead of $100,000. This was because of George.

Four large hotels had been built here, but they lost their shirts because we hadn't yet set up a bureau. After their failure, I asked all the cities to expend part of their income from room taxes to advertise and get an organization to bring conventions and tourists to our county. It is now working.

Medical Commissions and Committees

here were certain Board of Supervisors' committees that you had to take, and then there were others that you could do on your own if you wanted to. You weren't paid for those. I wanted to get on the health commissions because of incidents that had gotten me interested in health. I have already mentioned my wife's cancer early in our marriage.

My sister had married into a very old Sacramento family who knew the McClotskys who owned the newspapers and all that society. When we visited her in Squaw Valley, she said she wasn't feeling well. She had a pain in her side and had been to see the doctors. They did X-rays and tests and then wrote her off as a hypochondriac. I couldn't believe that there was nothing wrong with her. She had been a purser on the old Pan American China Clippers. Those were the seaplanes that used to go to Shanghai and all over the world. I knew she was a responsible person. I encouraged her to come and see my wife's doctor, Dr. Victor Richards. She agreed and came and stayed at our mother's house. I went to pick her up after her checkup and was feeling happy because I felt everything would be all right, and Dr. Richards would fix her up. I asked him how my sister, Betty, was.

"Well," he said, "I hate to tell you, but she has terminal cancer."

"Are you sure?" I asked.

He said, "I had nine colleagues of mine review this with me, and only one disagrees. I hope I'm wrong." Anyhow, she died about a year later.

These are some of the things that got me interested in health. I figured that I was so lucky having my wife come back like a miracle, that I should put something back into it, something for the health community. My philosophy is that whatever you put into anything you get back out. If you don't put anything into a relationship, you don't get anything. An old saying is, "Love is very shy. Love never goes where it's not invited and never stays where it's not wanted." If you put a lot in business, you get a lot out. If you put a lot in politics… I put a lot into politics and I got ten times as much back because I enjoyed practically every minute of it.

I got on all of these committees. I served as President of San Mateo County.

Comprehensive Health Planning Council

I was Vice-Chairman of the Bay Area Comprehensive Health Planning Council. I became President of the Health Service Agency for the United States government, which was to plan the health service in San Francisco, San Mateo and Marin Counties. The government also gave us several million dollars to develop that plan. I was also Director of a consortium to get better coordination among the six hospitals in San Mateo County, the Comprehensive Health Planning Council of San Mateo.

We realized, after a lot of debate, that we had to do so many different things and there wasn't enough money to support all these groups and to provide the health services that we hoped to provide. Our question was, "Where do we get the money?" If you think about it, you have three sources: patient fees, gifts and donations, grants or programs from the Federal government. Those are the only areas to get money. We had to figure out how much was needed, and how to purchase the best of what was most needed in our area. One idea was to see if the different groups like the Heart Association, the Lung Association, the TB Association and Easter Seals could get together and coordinate their spending programs in the community.

We were floundering around, and I guess a couple of weeks later a lady who was CEO of the TB Association called. We knew one another because six months before I had acted as Chairman of the Fund Drive that took in $250-300,000. This was more than they had ever before raised. I felt good about that, but I hate to ask for money, so I certainly wasn't going to do that again. I didn't enjoy it. She said they needed a new X-ray truck to go out and do screening. I asked her about the three or four trucks she had now. She insisted they needed another, and it would cost $90,000. She wanted me to ask the Board of Supervisors for a grant for the truck. I told her about the work we were doing on the Comprehensive Health Planning Council and asked her to come and justify her request before this group. The Board of Supervisors had put a lot of money into these services and we wanted to know which had most priority. She said to forget it; she wasn't going before the Council. She said, "We'll just go out and get our own money for it, we don't need you."

I said, "Thank you very much."

That attitude is still with me; it was totally unnecessary. I don't really like the TB Association now.

911 Health Program

There's a 911 Police Program, but there's also a 911 Health Program when an ambulance is called. I felt that we needed a 911 program and no one else really cared too much about it in San Mateo County. Not that they didn't care, that was a poor phrase. No one wanted to stick their neck our and ask for the money to support such a plan. It was very expensive. It cost hundreds of thousands of dollars. There were a lot of conflicts to resolve. There were ambulance people who had given contributions to many of the Councilmen throughout the County, and there were ambulance services in each of these cities. Most important, nobody wanted any changes, just like anything else. The Board felt that I was the health expert (not really expert, but nut or something), so they put it in my hands. We developed a program. We had some very capable technical people helping us from other areas, showing how the 911 program operated in their communities. They showed us what we would have to do to make it work. One thing that was needed after you got the ambulances, and the training of the people for emergency medicine to pick the people up, was a base hospital.

There were six hospitals and they all wanted to be the base hospital. There was enough commotion when we awarded the 911 emergency medical services to a group of professional ambulance people from Los Angeles. There were no professional, trained paramedics here to come in and immediately take over the program. That was a tough situation. We made a decision, and that was it. The next decision was about the base hospital.

Daly City was a real political haven and the Catholic Church was very important here. As a result, Mary's Help Hospital, which is now Seton Medical Center, wanted to be the base hospital. The Sister Superior asked the former mayor and political activists there, "Who do I see?" They told her to see Jim Fitzgerald. She asked that it be arranged, and I went to see her.

She was a gracious lady and she gave me all the arguments regarding their great facilities, location, etc. to be the base hospital. I had some questions for her. I had been on the Sewer Board, and some time ago we had sent some seriously injured people over to the emergency hospital at Mary's Help and there was no doctor on duty capable of caring for them. They had to be taken to another doctor's office. I found this totally unsatisfactory. Unless they changed that program, they were not going to be the base hospital. Whew!

She asked, "What do you suggest?"

I asked her to explain their present process. She said that they had a contract with the medical society in Northern San Mateo County, and she asked that I talk to them. I told her I'd be happy to have breakfast with them and she should let me know when she had arranged it. We met for breakfast and I got up and told them that we were going to appoint three hospitals as base hospitals, and the emergency medical facilities at Mary's Help were not adequate. Defending themselves, they explained that they had two doctors who took turns on call in the Emergency Room, sleeping there.

"Are they emergency medically trained?" I asked.

Their answer was unsatisfactory. They thought I was talking like some kind of nut.

Finally, after a lot of discussion reflecting the sort of lackadaisical attitude that doctors sometimes have – they really don't like to make changes or stick their necks out on anything – I said, "If you want this as an emergency base hospital, you have to develop a plan to be submitted to our technical people in the County. They'll go over the plan. It has to cover twenty-four hours a day, a plan that provides emergency medical service for most any type of emergency. You've got all these doctors here. There's no reason why you can't work something out to provide these services."

Well, after that I was like a leper.

Sister Superior called me later and said that she'd like me to come to her Board of Directors meeting at four o'clock the next day. I got there a bit early and was doodling around waiting for the meeting to start and the CEO of the hospital (nice man), comes over and whispers in my ear, "Jim, what you're doing is one hundred per cent right. However, I am not going to vote for your plan today."

I couldn't believe what I was hearing. He went over and sat down next to Sister Superior and everybody got up and talked. I got up and gave my spiel without any reaction. After the meeting, I went over to the Sister and told her this was ridiculous, and told her what had happened. I said that this was not a matter of politics, but health and emergency services. Maybe she didn't understand this.

"You have a good program here. You have a good location, and I'm sure we'd like to make you a base hospital, but your services here stink. You don't have an emergency medical department."

She didn't say anything, but thanked me. I left and I guess it was about a week later that she called and said they had changed their whole program. They had contracted with a group of qualified, certified emergency medical doctors.

That is how things are in politics. Fortunately, Sister Superior realized and did the right thing. Later she invited my wife, Jean, and me to a Christmas party at the World Trade Center. It was a beautiful party. If you think you've been to parties, go to a Seton Hospital cocktail party. It was unbelievably good!

Hospital Coordination

A little later, I could see that some of the hospitals did not have enough volume in certain specialties. One hospital, for example would have two or three births a month, while others had thirty. Checking it out, the experts say there is no way you could have a good specialist care with only two patients a month. You need to have two or three a *day* to keep up your skills and have all the supplies you need there. What we had was duplication, and it was very costly. I thought I'd have some fun, so I brought it up at a Board of Supervisors meeting, and suggested the Board coordinate all hospitals. It was ridiculous, because we had no authority to do that. They knew what a nut I was, so they came back with a program to form a sort of consortium to coordinate the six hospitals. Each hospital would be represented, and the Board of Supervisors and they would discuss how we could better coordinate delivery of hospital care. I thought this was good. I took my wife with me down to the dinner they had at the Peninsula Hospital. I didn't get to see her too much during these days. The dinner was the best thing you could have. It was like a five star restaurant in Paris. They had wine and the whole ball of wax. After dinner we started talking and it was all resolved. Maybe one hospital would take care of, say, pediatrics, even though people would scream about it. At that time there were not so many babies.

We were going along, accomplishing some minor things. Then someone suggested, I guess it was me, that the County Hospital Coordinator, who worked for private hospitals, had nothing to do for about six months. In fact, he'd be interested in taking over coordinating the work that we were doing among our six hospitals. That's wonderful, to have an expert like that who would run fifty or one hundred hospitals in the private sector. A few weeks after that beautiful dinner, I asked that man, "If you are in a private hospital, how much money do you have to make for the people who own the hospital?"

He said, "Thirty per cent."

I said, "How come we have so much trouble here with cost, and we don't make any profit?"

When I asked the administrators of all our hospitals how come we weren't making a profit, they said that nobody ever asked them to make a profit or to cut their services to make a profit.

Amazing! I guess that the doctors are the ones who are salesmen. They bring in the patients to hospitals. You can't get into a hospital, except through emergency, without a doctor referring you. At least that's the way it used to be. If doctors don't refer you to a particular hospital, that hospital won't do any business. What the hospitals do to get business is to provide scanners and every up-to-date machine that's imaginable to the doctors, so they will bring their patients there. To me, it's wonderful that every hospital has the best facilities; that's good. But the question later comes up, "Is it necessary?"

The Health Service Agency

The Federal government, the State and we in San Mateo County taking our own survey, found out that the occupancy of the hospitals was fifty per cent and each one of those hospital beds, with the facilities provided at that time, cost over $100,000. If you had a hundred beds and it cost you $5,000 a day to run the hospital, you could charge $50 a bed if you had one hundred per cent occupancy. If you had fifty per cent occupancy, you would have to charge $100 a bed. In a hospital, it's like the police department and everything else, you have to provide a twenty-four-hour service. Even though it's not that many patients, you still can't reduce your costs a great deal, with everybody buying those scanners at $250,000, and all the other special equipment. The Federal government under the Carter Administration, I think, was getting prepared for a National Health Insurance. All the different areas in the country had to have a Health Service Agency. Our area consisted of Marin, San Francisco, and San Mateo Counties. I was a delegate to the Health Service Agency. On the agency in our area, we had forty-nine per cent doctors and providers and fifty-one per cent consumers, people not in the medical field I was considered a provider, even though I didn't provide anything, but because I was in government. I was Vice-President, and the President was the President of the telephone company.

We had thirty-five openings for this particular commission. Everybody and his uncle wanted to be on this, every doctor, every nurse, every dentist. It was incredible, the number of activists and all that kind of stuff. The President of the agency had never been in politics. We would go until two o'clock in the morning, trying to find out who was going to be seated and who was not. In the early hours of the morning, we would vote on a thing that was of interest to the doctors, and then they would go home. About 12 or 1 A.M. the activists who didn't like the doctors would bring it up again and change the vote on it! It was just screwy. At the end of about two years, we got thirty-five people seated. We sent the list to Dr. Feinstein of the Federal government. He wrote a six-page letter stating that we were not in conformity of Section 4068 and Section 2423, etc. He came to the meeting and told us we were being given two more weeks to get ourselves into conformity.

The President got very upset and wanted to get out of this mess, so he resigned. I was the first Vice-President. The second Vice President was a black man who was the CEO of San Francisco General Hospital. This is a true story, but no one believes it. I said to everybody that I'd send them a letter and tell them what they had to do to get in compliance and if they agreed, see Mr. Windsor, who was the second Vice-President. Let him know, and we'll have a meeting in two weeks. If you don't agree with the items in the letter, then we're not going to have a meeting. But first I had to find out what we needed to do. I said to Dr. Feinstein, "Can you come over to the San Franciscan Hotel on Market Street? I'd like to ask you a few things, and we could have an Irish coffee, on me."

We went over there and ordered Irish Coffee and chatted about a few things. Then we got to business, and I said, "I don't understand this Section 4068 and 2423 and that kind of stuff."

"Well," he said, "In a nutshell, it means that you have too many blacks on your committee."

"What else?" I asked.

He said, "That's it. That's all there is. You've got to get rid of some blacks."

"Why do we have to get rid of some blacks? We knocked our brains out finding qualified blacks so that no one could say they weren't represented."

He said, "No, the demographics survey shows that there's only 8.6% blacks, and you have 15% blacks proportionate on the committee."

So I went to Charlie Windsor, who I guess is the only black who has been to my house for dinner and is a really wonderful guy, and told him, "It's up to you. You've got to get rid of some blacks and then we have to hire some people and spend about a million bucks."

He said, "We don't want to spend the money."

I said, "I know that. But they want us to spend the money and they want us to get this plan out and we have to get in conformity. But I'm going to Aspen, Colorado."

I had this date for about six months to go to Aspen. I told him I'd phone in and see if the meeting was on, and if it was fine. I phoned, and sure enough, he had a meeting and everybody agreed. We hired all these people and started to make this big health plan.

When I was running the commission, the meetings ended about 9:30 or 10 P.M. I had an agenda, and once an item was voted on, we wouldn't take it up again at that meeting. Soon it was time for another election. The activists all whispered around that I was too conservative and was appointing all my friends to the committee, and it was just terrible, what I was doing. So Charlie Windsor asked me to come down to the San Francisco Tennis Club with him and meet with this group. I guess they went to him because he was black. He and I went down there and had a meeting with this group. They said, "You're appointing all your friends."

I said, "I don't have any friends that I have appointed. Who are you talking about? Here's a list of names I've appointed. This one was recommended to my by Dr. Wang and the executive committee, and the three of you are on the executive committee. You suggested this person, and so-and-so suggested this person. I haven't even suggested anyone. Anything else?"

Well, that was the end of the meeting, and they elected me to be President. Not that they were happy about it, but we went ahead and tried to develop this plan. We were being pushed to get the plan together. Every time the committee had any suggestions to fix anything, we were told we didn't have the authority to do it. Here was a case where we were members of a governmentally appointed committee to put our name on this thing and it wasn't even our plan. Unfortunately, no one's ever even seen it, and millions and millions of dollars were spent all over the country. We spent about $4 million just in our little area. This is just one case where money gets wasted.

At this time, if anybody wanted to buy one of those expensive pieces of equipment, they had to come before our organization, the Health Service Agency. If a hospital wanted to expand, it had to come before our organization. And our organization tried to develop and consolidate hospitals, and reduce the cost of delivering health care. We didn't want every doctor's office to have a $250,000 scanning machine. I can see some merit in this kind of thing.

The crazy part about this is that the logical place to eliminate was St. Joseph's Hospital. We all agreed on that and suggested St. Joseph's Hospital be shut down. Well, it was shut down, and who should be working there, but my daughter, Susan Fitzgerald. She was drawing blood at St. Joseph's. She had a degree in Medical Technology, but she was having a tough time finding a job. She had to have intern training, so this was her start. The professor at her college helped her find another job at old Stanford Hospital in San Francisco, which then changed to Presbyterian, and now is California Pacific Hospital, which is part of old Children's Hospital and Presbyterian. It was a good thing, and worked out well for her in the long run.

ABAG

I was also Director of the Association of the Bay Area Governments. This is a group of governments. There are several hundred cities in the Bay Area, and all kinds of governmental jurisdictions that belong to ABAG. I was also Chairman of the Emergency Health Service Committee. Usually ABAG was known as "Windbag" to the people, because they just talked and there was never any conclusion on any of the problems. On the Emergency Medical Committee there were several supervisors who I had known through the years. There was one lady, a supervisor from San Francisco, who I had not known, and I thought she had different ideas from mine. I thought we were different in many ways. But in the particular situation, she had the same thoughts that I had and we agreed on almost everything. She was an attorney and divorced, and she had to bring her son to the meetings. I felt sorry for this poor little guy, seven or eight years of age, staying up until midnight for the meetings and then going home. She didn't get re-elected.

The difficulty that arose was that the Emergency Medical Services, the 911 programs which we had in most of the counties surrounding the Bay, had produced a problem. The Bay Area is like a saucer with mountains around it. When you send out a radio beam, it can bounce off the mountains and it can go a different way from what we want it to go. This caused a problem with the ambulances when they were bringing heart patients to the hospital. They would use the radio to pass on the vital information to the hospital and the various signals would get mixed up. This was unacceptable. We checked it out to determine how we were going to work this out. We decided we should buy this super computer, locate it in San Mateo County and program it so that my heartbeat would go to the right hospital and wouldn't be mixed up with Joe Doak's heartbeat and vital information. We knew we needed to put some money up for this.

Nobody complained. They all put up money and it ended up where there were about ninety different organizations, hospitals, cities and counties that not only paid for the computer, but signed contracts to pay their portion of the maintenance and operation of it. That was something! I don't think ABAG ever made an arrangement or had such agreement. When you talk about health, you cross political boundaries. But when I think about it, that's not really accurate, if you think of what is going on in Washington.

North Coast Sanitary District

Another agency that I was a director of was the North Coast Sanitary District, which is a sewerage district. It was in the heart of Daly City located in a park. Part of it was underground. That was an education! When I got on there with a couple of other people, we wanted to clean the place up and we felt that we didn't want any odors coming out of it and we really wanted to clean the sewage up so the water would eventually be drinkable. That was the plan. We were dedicated to that. That was called "tertiary treatment". Sometimes dreams never come true. The first thing we did was to get all the workers clean white overalls, and we made them get shots so that they wouldn't be ill if they messed with the sewage, which they could easily do every day. The operation of the plant was quite interesting. Most people don't even want to hear about it, but this is the way it is.

The sewage comes down in this big pipe to the plant and there are screens there to take out the rubber goods, rags, and all kinds of extras like bricks that are unsuitable for the plant. The screened out residue is trucked out and disposed of. After the sewage is screened, it goes into what is called a settling pond. This is where the solids go down to the bottom of the tank and the water surfaces to the top. This effluent is taken off. The solids are pumped into a big tank that hold all of these little bugs, the same bugs we have in our own stomachs. The temperature of the bugs in these tanks have to be kept at body temperature or the bugs die and the sewage is not eaten up. There are some things the bugs don't like, like eggshells and coffee grounds and sand. Before the solids go in the tanks, this extraneous matter is taken out. If the bugs are healthy, about ninety per cent of the solid sewage is eaten. The bugs give off ethane gas, and in the sewer plant vehicles can run on this gas.

A lot of people are proposing using this gas. The trouble in a car is the residue from this gas. Of course, there is plenty of it around. Most of it is burned off. So the effluent that is eventually going into the ocean goes into another tank and oxygen is pumped throughout the effluent and most of the germs are killed. I never realized that when you have crashing waterfalls and streams that the oxygen helps purify the water. So this is what happens here; you purify the water. If you haven't killed all the germs, in another tank they pour chlorine (like Clorox) into it. It's the same thing that you use in pools to clean them. After that it goes into another tank to remove the chlorine before you can dispose of it in the ocean.

By this time, this has become pretty good water. It hasn't any bugs, it's very clear. It isn't drinkable, but it could be reused. We thought it was crazy to go to all this trouble just to pump it out to sea. We ought to have a use for it because it's not contaminated. You can't get sick on it, but psychologically, you wouldn't want to use it on food plants you are going to consume.

There are many golf courses and cemeteries in this area. The idea was that we could build a big tank and we'd put this effluent in it and reuse it on the golf courses. The average golf course uses a million to two million gallons of pure drinking water to irrigate it. That's a waste of beautiful clear drinking water. The Olympic Club gave us a site where we could put this tank. It was a million-gallon tank. We talked to the cemetery people and they indicated they would go along with using it for the lawns at the cemeteries. We built the tank, and everything was going great, and all of a sudden after it's built, the cemetery people say they don't want the effluent. They don't want to pay for the pipes to bring it over, even though it would be cheaper than water. The cemeteries use five or six inches of water per month for their lawns. It would have been a great recycling project.

When I left, I don't know what happened to the concept. At least we tried, and that's what is going to have to happen in the future. You can't waste good drinking water on golf courses and cemetery lawns.

Bay Area Sewage Service Agency

Because I was on the North County Sanitary District, they appointed me to be on the Bay Area Sewage Service Agency. This was a State group that was to clean up San Francisco Bay. They made me chairman of the Planning Committee. At that time, we had, as President, Norman Minetta, who was a Congressman, and he had been for quite a while. Dianne Feinstein was Secretary. We had three Supervisors: Mendelson, Gonzales and Molinari from San Francisco. This was an education in politics! It was crazy. The meeting started at 7:30, but Mendelson, Gonzales and Molinari would come at 8:30 eating ice cream cones. We were paid $50 a meeting. Everybody else was pretty serious about it because we had around three billion dollars to OK to try to clean up the Bay.

Molinari gets up and says, "Where do we have the bank account?"

Minetta says, "Mrs. Feinstein put it in her bank."

"Whose attorney are we using?"

"We're using Mrs. Feinstein's attorney."

There were other questions, and it was, "Mrs. Feinstein took care of that."

The next meeting they all got there early, and I knew something was cooking here. They were all smiling and they said that we had twenty members of this board and in San Francisco they had eleven members on the Board of Supervisors. So the organization there is more efficient. You can't have this many people taking care of things without a rules committee. Us naive characters, we didn't even know what the rules committee was, because we never had a rules committee before. But in Sacramento and Washington, D.C., they know what it is. So Minetta appoints Molinari as chairman of the rules committee, and he chooses Mendelson and Gonzales to serve on the committee. Then at the next meeting, Minetta asks for a report.

They made a report, and what it amounted to was that Supervisor Feinstein didn't have any authority. They changed the ball game and took away all of her authority. I think that was the last we saw of Mrs. Feinstein at those meetings. She had taken over and they didn't like it, and they gave her some San Francisco politics. We got into threatening everybody if they didn't get into the program and clean up their part of the Bay, that we'd take over their sewage agency and we would run it. We had that authority from the State to do it. Pretty soon we were getting all these plants cleaning up their acts.

I got carried away about trying to clean up San Francisco Bay. I found the different problems unbelievable, such as half or more of the State has tributaries with sewage and all kinds of stuff dumped into the Sacramento and San Joaquin rivers coming in to San Francisco Bay. I realized it was a Herculean project that certainly the cities and counties couldn't solve alone. The Federal Government should come in and help us. They sent me back to a County Supervisor's Convention and I was to give a talk on the problem of the drainage in the San Francisco Bay basin. The Federal government representative was there.

I gave my talk, and the Federal official, who was very knowledgeable, said, "Mr. Fitzgerald, you are entirely right. The problem is here, and we haven't really made people do anything about it. The sewage and storm drainage that goes out into the Bay from all the cities, the people spitting on sidewalks, the dog debris, cattle manure from dairies, and all that stuff is something that we just haven't addressed. We are going to have a sewage study program, a Clean Water Program. There's nothing we can do right now."

What happened was that I got appointed to this Clean Water Program (they always like to say "clean water" rather than sewage) as the Western States Representative. I was the only one there from California. We went all over the United States having these meetings. The idea was, how do you stop every pollutant from getting into the streams? How do you take care of getting rid of manure from the dairies, etc.? It was a gigantic problem. The funny thing about it is that San Francisco, which has one of the oldest sewage systems, was actually far ahead of anybody in the United States.

The City of San Bruno, like all the other cities, has storm drains that are separate from the sewer pipes that go into the sewer treatment plants, so when anything happens, the storm drains go right into the Bay without any treatment. But in San Francisco, the storm drains and the sewer are one. Being one is the problem that San Francisco had. How do you clean up all that sewage and storm drainage that comes down when it rains? They found a solution. When you go out to the zoo, they've built this gigantic treatment plant. It has a huge tank underneath the Great Highway that goes for miles. When it rains, the sewage can be impounded in the tank. They can treat so many million gallons an hour until they treat the whole capacity of the tank. So the raw sewage and storm water is not going out into the ocean anymore until it is all treated. That plant is probably one of the best in the world.

Sick Leave

I had always worked for myself and didn't get paid for holidays and things, but County employees got fourteen days of sick leave plus three or four weeks of vacation with pay. I found out that out of the 5,000 or more employees, everybody was taking their fourteen sick days each year, whether they were sick or not. It was a very sickly group! This amounted to three or four million dollars a year to pay for the temporary help. I inaugurated a policy that may still be in use today. If you did not take your sick days, when you retire from the County, we will pay one year's free health insurance for every year you didn't use your fourteen days. You would have to be with the County for at least ten years to qualify for this. What happened as a result was that nobody was taking their sick leave unless they were sick. The bad part was that some people were coming to work sick. It sounded like a great idea at the time. Health insurance was cheap then.

BART

This started before I was on the Board of Supervisors, so it must have been before 1960. There was a group of big businessmen from Kaiser, Chevron and all the big companies around the Bay Area who decided there should be a rapid transit system around the perimeter of San Francisco Bay. They devised a plan without any input, as far as I know, from the elected officials who were going to have to dig up the money. The local officials had some input, but it was ignored. They had this plan that BART would run from San Francisco under the Golden Gate to Marin County, around Marin to Sonoma, then over to Richmond and out to Lafayette and Walnut Creek, and then come down and go absolutely around the Bay through San Jose and up through Santa Clara and San Mateo Counties back to San Francisco. It was a loop rail system which, of course, is best because there's no deadheading – meaning they don't have to stop and turn around. This way it can just keep going around in a circle. It sounded great, of course. The cost was in the billions of dollars, so it was a very important decision to make. We started to look at it, but it was very complicated for me.

We had Louie Chess on the Board. He had run a railroad, the Southern Pacific, and had become the manager for the whole Western United States. So he was an expert on this issue. When we talked to the people on these committees making the plans, they said the trains would go 125 miles an hour on the open stretch, as long as they didn't have to stop. If you stop to pick up people, the best you can do is fifty-five or sixty miles per hour. They said with the special gauge track they could do this.

Louie asked, "What kind of special gauge?"

They said, "It's not standard gauge, it's special."

In other words, it's not the same as any other trains in the United States; it will be specific for BART. There will be nothing you can connect to, none of the other Southern Pacific, Northern

Pacific or Santa Fe systems. There would be no way to interchange trains.

This was the first problem. We decided we had better look at financing and see what was going on. We called Government Research, which is a non-profit agency in San Mateo County. They had experts from the telephone company and Standard Oil and Raytheon and all different big companies in the County. The chairman was Charlie Irelton, who was a vice-president of Pacific Telephone Company. They found that in financing, Marin County didn't have enough assessed valuation to support their share of the cost allotted to them. They found that Santa Clara County was not going into the system. That meant there was no loop around the Bay. The old railroad man, Louie, said you don't want to deadhead, because you lost money and time and everything else. So he proposed they go across the Dumbarton Bridge to make a loop. At that time they planned to go over the San Francisco/Oakland Bay Bridge or under it, so there would still be a loop, but it would miss San Jose because it was in Santa Clara County.

They said, "No, we don't want that." Southern Pacific said that regardless of where BART had their stations, they would still run their SP trains from San Jose to San Francisco. That screwed things up. Then the Government Research people found that the Marin County share of the cost was going to have to be picked up by San Mateo County. We complained about this, but nothing was done. Then the two billion of the three billion was not going to be enough to complete the system, and because San Mateo County had a train service from San Jose to San Francisco, San Mateo County would be the last on the list for BART construction.

If San Mateo had an election to approve of BART, there was so much anti-BART feeling and voter apathy and so forth, it probably would kill any chance that BART would get off the ground. We thrashed this around and voted not to give it to the people for a vote, but opt out. The powerful interests promoting this plan were able to change the voting requirement from 66 2/3% to 50%, if I remember right. When the election did come about, it passed by about 51%. As soon as this happened, they changed the plan. They said it wasn't feasible to put the train on the Golden Gate Bridge to Marin County. They ran out of money, so there was no money to extend BART down to San Mateo County. Then San Francisco came up with a plan to run BART directly to the Airport for only $90 million. We thought it would be a great idea if it cost only $90 million. It would be a surface train direct to the airport. By the time we got finished and everybody got what they wanted, BART wanted $500 million to connect with it. Even on that basis, they were going to soak the travelers that come in and out of San Francisco so much money to pay for the costs. It didn't work out, so everything sort of died. That was a long time ago. Now, of course it has been revived.

At that time, Southern Pacific trains were carrying about eight or nine thousand passengers a day. We did all kinds of things to get people to ride the trains. The traffic on Bayshore wasn't like today, and they were working on plans for a southern Bay crossing from East Bay to Army Street in San Francisco. There was to be a Bayfront freeway out in the Bay directly to San Jose. There would be yacht clubs and so forth along the westerly side of the freeway. Some part was to be on fill and others on bridges, so there would be water circulation. Then the 280 Highway was just being finished, and there were all these feelings that there was plenty of room on the freeways, and people in San Mateo County had no problems in getting to and from where they wanted to go. It was not like today. The people of San Mateo County even voted down a bond issue to put bypasses on all the Southern Pacific crossings so there would be no signals and delays due to trains. That idea was killed, and the people just didn't want any more taxes. So there we are.

This was an interesting time because I met such interesting people like Martin Wonderlich and Bill Bottoms, and people from the Crocker Land Company. Crocker Land is McKesson Robbins – Foremost McKesson, now. That's the big drug manufacturer and holding company. It was by meeting Martin Wonderlich and becoming friendly with him that I started sort of taxing his brains. When I had some problems with the County, I'd go over and talk to him. Although he had no advanced education like college, this guy was a genius. He looked like he didn't know the time of day.

He was about 6'4" and weighed about 240 pounds. He didn't say much, but kept everything very simple. When I told him I was having this problem with BART and asked him what to do with it and the five feet of paper studies and so forth that they gave me. I'd read a lot of it, and I'd listened to people, and I was having a hard time understanding what they were saying. I wanted to know if I was dumb. He said, "Well the secret is, if they don't know how to explain it to you, they don't really know what they are talking about. If you can't understand what they are talking about, then you don't do anything."

It was so logical. We became friends.

The Fitzgerald Marine Reserve

As things went along, the Board of Supervisors made me the chairman. I was made chairman five times in the twenty years, which was a lot. During that time, I worked very hard on different projects. One of the early ones was the Marine Reserve.

Because I was in the real estate business, the Fitzgerald Marine Reserve evolved. I was diving there with a friend of mine, who was the building inspector of San Bruno. We'd go over there and dive for abalone. I didn't really know how to dive, but we got these rubber suits because it was so cold. We figured out a system so we could get a few abalone. It was a lot of fun but a lot of work. I went over to the coast and people got to know who I was and so forth.

They told me, "Listen, we're not going to be able to come down here any more because Senator McAteer, Gene McAteer, is buying up all the property on the beach here, and we won't be able to get through to the water."

I was a supervisor at this time. I checked it out and there was a piece of property for sale for about $3,000. It was a lot with entrance to what is now the Fitzgerald Marine Reserve. I got the County to buy that piece of property, thinking everybody should be able to use it, my diving friends and anyone who wants to come down and see the tide pools. What happened was that the schools heard about it and on low tide days, they brought about 4,000 little kids with buckets and plastic bags and just picked off from the reef what was exposed: crab, snails, starfish and the whole works. When this happened, the environmentalists went nuts, and they determined that this couldn't continue because the children were taking everything and destroying it. They decided it would be better if the reef was left without anybody being able to go there. I thought I'd get a bunch of my diving buddies and go out to another reef and we'd replenish it. They went nuts again, and said we couldn't do that, bringing foreign material onto this reef. It was the worst thing.

I remembered from my real estate days that the beaches to the high tide mark belong to the State of California. It took us about sixteen years, but with the aid of our lobbyist, Mr. George Potroff, we got the State Legislature to make that a reserve. After all those years, they named it the Fitzgerald Marine Reserve after me. It didn't cost any money because the State owns the land underneath the water. It took that length of time to work out a satisfactory deal. We wanted to make it a preservation area so you couldn't take anything. The fishermen protested and in order to get it through, we had to OK the taking of abalone and eels. But you can't take a rock!

Henry Doelger owned some property at Uplands that he sold to Westinghouse Electric Company. Westinghouse owned a golf course in Half Moon Bay and they wanted to put in another golf course. The County owned a group of tax deeded lots. They were all over the place, and some were in the center of the development where Westinghouse wanted to put the golf course. We traded these lots for the property above the Marine Reserve, so now there are headlands where you can walk through the trees and look onto the beaches. It is a very beautiful place.

Marine Reserve – kids investigating a tide pool

Jim at Fitzgerald Marine Reserve

Marine Reserve Investigating Tide Pool

Redwood Trees, Huppart Park Creek

Redwood Hiking Trail, Huppart Park

Marine Reserve – Sea Animals

Marine Reserve – More Sea Animals

The Marine Reserve at Low Tide

Tidal pool, Virginia Welch

Diving and the South Pacific

My fascination with the water and the South Pacific started when I was about eight or nine years old. My mother took me to see Ramon Navarro in *The Pagan Love Song*. He was in the South Pacific and he was under a banana tree and reaching up with his toes pulling down these bananas to eat, and the waves were crashing on the shore. Then, when I was in the Navy, I was sent to Oahu in Hawaii. I spent two years there and had the opportunity to dive in the tropical waters. The fish and coral were beautiful, even though I only had Japanese pearl diver's wooden glasses to use. I could see a lot of fish at Hanauma Bay, which is now a marine reserve.

At the time, Jacques Cousteau had written a book called *The Silent World*. He was the man who invented the aqualung when Nazi Germany occupied France. The tales he told in the book about getting a thirty-pound lobster and being able to swim like a fish absolutely fascinated me.

In later years, after I was elected to the Board of Supervisors, I wanted to go diving. I bought a wetsuit, but didn't buy any weights. I finally decided I'd better take some lessons. Ed Brawley was a fantastic teacher. He had a classroom where we would talk about catching lobster and scallops. He had me so excited my eyes were popping out of my head. He gave us lectures on what not to touch, what to do and what not to do. Finally we went down to Carmel, near where the Carmelite Nuns are located. There's a beautiful beach there. It was cold and we put on our wetsuits and our weights. In free diving, the idea is to dive fifteen feet down and pick up something and you pass the test. I was fascinated because this was all cold water, not like Hawaii, yet there were these beautiful fronds of seaweed, like a forest. I passed the test. Once I was just playing in the water, and I had a buddy there with me. All of a sudden some seaweed got loose and wrapped around my neck and I was practically drowning. My buddy took the seaweed off me. It goes to show that you have to have a buddy. That's the system, of course; when you're diving, you have a buddy. It's hard to find a good buddy who is going to take care of you.

There was a doctor who was in charge of mental health in San Mateo County. He was a nice young fellow and I liked him a great deal. I could see that he was very troubled. About this time, I decided I wanted to get into scuba-diving, diving with tanks. Ed Brawley had a program for it. I talked to the doctor and told him it would do him some good to try it, too. We went to Ed Brawley's class in the pool at the Veterans Memorial Building in San Francisco. We went through all the diving. He had us swim underwater without taking a breath, and you had to do all kinds of stuff. The doctor was about six feet tall and 200 pounds. In the pool, we were supposed to go down, one person lay on the bottom and the other one is supposed to rescue him, pick him up, and flip him onto an inner tube. My buddy was the doctor, so I went down first. He came down, picked me up and unceremoniously dumped me onto the inner tube, and I got some water in my nose and down my throat. He decided to go down for his turn immediately. So he's down there, lying on the bottom of the pool, and I haven't even got my breath yet. I decided to go down before he drowns, because he's really into this thing. I go down, and remember, he's 200 pounds. I pick him up and get him up. With all my strength and the help of the buoyancy of the water, I get him onto the inner tube. He's just pretending to be limp and slides off the goddamn inner tube and goes back down to the bottom of the pool. I'm so tired now, I can hardly see! I finally had to go back down and get him on the inner tube again.

As a side issue, later on I heard that he was down in Zihuatanejo with Dr. Timothy Leary, and they were trying LSD, a new hallucinogenic drug. I was unhappy with this, so I contacted him and asked what he was doing down there using illegal drugs. He was very conscientious and said, "We use alcohol in the mental health field. We're trying to find out what's really wrong with the people, and using this hallucinogenic we might be able to straighten somebody out." He said he was down there to be a physician in case something went wrong. He said something did go wrong when Dr. Leary took LSD and ran into barbed wire and scratched himself all over, and they had to restrain him. I guess you've heard about Timothy Leary and how he was never the same after those drugs.

I got busy and unfortunately couldn't complete the course to get a certification, which was good. Not being a certified diver meant that any time I went scuba-diving, I had to go through exercises and skills tests before I did any diving. I think this is good because if you are certified, it could be a couple of years between dives, and you might think you know everything. I've run across some of these certified divers and I'm uncertified, and I must say, I am better than them.

We went to Hawaii and we were on the island of Maui visiting some friends. I decided to take a leave of absence and take a scuba-diving jaunt. When I told the dive boat people that I wanted to go scuba-diving, they asked me if I had been certified. I said no, so they took me in the water and put me through the paces and found out that I knew a little bit about what I was doing, so they accepted me. We hopped on the boat and went up around Maui and went diving about 25-30 feet. We saw coral and fish and it was really fantastic. It was a beautiful day and the people I met were good company. That's half the fun of it. People are all very friendly and the camaraderie is excellent. Once in a while you find some kook, but normally you don't. They were going out the next day. I asked if they were going to stay in the nice shallow water.

They said yes, so I asked if I could go along. They said, "Yeah, you've got it all together, no problem, you know how to scuba-dive."

Next morning we hopped into this small boat without a cabin. It was pouring rain, just an absolute tropical storm. There were about eight of us on the deck with our wetsuits on while the rain was pouring down on us. Off we went to the island of Lanai. I had a new gadget, a depth gauge.

When we got there is was so stormy the boat was rocking like the dickens and the dive master said, "If you stay here, you're going to get sick. The worst thing you can do is throw up in your mask."

That was enough for me. We all hopped over and were going to go down the anchor rope. I started down the rope. At ten feet I was clearing my ears, and then it was fifteen and then twenty feet. All of a sudden, it was thirty-five feet, then forty-five. I had never been there before. It got to fifty-five feet, sixty-five, then eighty five to ninety feet.

We went into this cave of coral, called the Cathedral. We went in and looked up and you could see through the coral and the manta rays and schools of fish. You don't even know there's a storm up above. It's quiet. There were about seven of us in there. I noticed our leader was pulling out his knife, and I wondered what was going on. Then I saw the shark. It wasn't the biggest shark in the world, but it was a shark and it seemed about six feet long. I thought, Oh, my God. The girl next to her boyfriend and me was having trouble with her mask and I really thought she was going to take off out of the cave. I thought the shark would bite her in the rear end and I was going to have to help fight the shark to try to save her. I came to the realization that this was what I'd have to do, and that was it. It was a very important moment in my life.

The next thing I know, the shark is gone, and she's OK and everybody is going into this cave, which is about three feet in diameter. With our tanks, that was a tight space. I was the last one to go in and I couldn't see in front of me enough to know if the person in front of me was going to kick my respirator out of my mouth. I had my hands in front of my face so they couldn't kick my mask out. Well, I'm going through this cave at eighty-five feet and saying to myself, "This is the nuttiest thing I have ever done."

All of a sudden, there in a little part of the cave is our leader with the light. He's motioning me to go, so I go, and it's like a lava tube that just shoots you right out into this beautiful water. You could just see forever, it seemed. We swam and swam over mounds and down dales, going from sixty to thirty feet. You have to adjust your ears, so you go back to forty and sixty again. Finally, we realize that we have about 500 pounds of air left, so our leader points to go up to the surface.

On the surface it's stormy, the boat is rocking. There's a ladder on the side. The boat is fifteen to twenty five feet or less.

When I got on the ladder, a wave hit and picked me and the ladder up and threw me on the bottom of the boat on my stomach and head. The ladder is smashed and my head is bleeding. It wasn't too bad, so we went to a place that is not so deep. Everybody was looking at me and can see that I'm bleeding. I know they're thinking to themselves that I've screwed up the deal and they're going to have to go home and they're not going to get their second dive in. The leader patched my head up with a few Band-Aids and we went for another dive.

It was still rough; this time there's no ladder to get into the boat. The waves were cracking, so you had to step on the outboard motor to get in. I'll tell you, my respirator came off and I got a gulp of salt water. Thank goodness, I put my snorkel back in and I was able to get some air. They then pulled me into the boat.

That was my first real dive and that was at the Cathedral of the island of Lanai. What a beautiful place! I hope they haven't messed that up. I went for many scuba dives in Hawaii. I had made arrangements with Maui divers to go diving, but I had to cancel because I had a cold. You're not supposed to dive if you have a cold because you can't clear your ears. After about six days I felt I had pretty well gotten rid of the cold or hay fever or whatever it was. I took off with Maui divers on another rainy, rainy day. The boat took about fifty people; it was a beautiful big boat. Only one other person showed up for the dive. Everyone else had canceled out. The Captain was there to drive the boat and a woman who served the pawpaws and also did the diving. So we were sitting there talking with this young gentleman, who was about thirty-two years old and in good shape. He commented that it sounded like I had a cold. I said that I did have one. He inquired if I was going to go diving. I said I was going to try, but if I couldn't clear my ears I wouldn't dive, but just stay on the boat. He asked if I took any Sudafed, and I said I never took any of that. My instructor, Ed Brawley, had said that if you're going to go diving, you don't go with a cold and you don't take any medicine like Sudafed or the likes.

The young man said he was an emergency medical doctor and he said he always took Sudafed before he took a dive. This surprised me. He said he took Afrin. He offered me some Afrin and some Sudafed to clear myself off. So I did, and it cleared it up. Since there were only four of us, they decided to take some pictures, and wanted me to hop in. I did, but instead of putting my snorkel in my mouth, I had put my regulator in and I began to use air. They were fooling around and finally the other three got in. My buddy was the Captain, and the doctor's buddy was the girl. We went down to about 115 feet, and we were looking at this black coral and gorgeous orange and pink fish. We were only down there about fifteen minutes when I noticed that I only had about 500 pounds of air left. I had gone through almost 2,000 pounds of air in fifteen minutes, so I am really taking the air in.

I tapped the Captain and gave him the sign across my throat, meaning my air is going out. So he came to me and points me in the direction of the boat and leaves me. This is absolutely terrible. All of a sudden I got what is called a reverse squeeze. I can't clear my ears and it's starting to hurt. I went up to twenty feet and they're just really painful. I went down again, trying to get rid of this and doing everything, squishing my nose, pump my ears to equalize them from the change in depth, and can't do it. Finally, I looked at my tank and noticed I had a hundred pounds of air and I was going to drown if I didn't get up. The pain was excruciating, and I swam up as fast as I could and grabbed the ladder to get on the boat. Normally I don't go up the ladder with the tank on my back. I always have someone take it off. Well, I had just enough strength to get out of there, and it hurt so bad that I just got up and almost ran up the ladder.

My ears were really hurting. When the rest of our party got back I told them what had happened. So the doctor suggested I go to see a doctor. I went to the doctor with my ears bleeding a little bit. He gave me holy hell. He said, "You're absolutely stupid. I don't understand why anybody does any diving to wreck themselves like this. You're lucky you didn't break your eardrums. You almost did."

The next day I took it easy. The doctor who had been on the dive took a bus and traveled around the island to see how I was. He was a nice guy, but it goes to show you, I broke the rules. Don't ever go diving with a cold!

I mentioned some of the problems that you can have when you're diving, but most of the time you have such a wonderful time. We were at the Moana Kea Hotel Beach, and I decided to take a refresher course in scuba-diving, so I signed up and came down to the beach at about eight o'clock in the morning. I saw this lady there, a beautiful lady with long black hair, very tanned, wearing a bikini. I asked, "Are you my instructor?"

She laughed and said, "No, I'm your buddy."

Then the instructor came, and he was blond, very light, and a Stanford graduate. We went out and went through the various drills, clearing your mask, taking the regulator out of your mouth, and so forth. The girl's name was Louise, and she was having a difficult time clearing her mask. The next day we went out on the boat and we took a dive and were down about twenty-five feet. She was getting water in her mask, so I was helping her. We both passed the examination and we came back in, and she said, "How about having a cocktail after dinner tonight?"

When we were going into the dining room, she yells over, "Hi, Jim!" And she says to everybody, "There's my buddy."

So we had dinner and we went to the cocktail lounge and I was talking to her husband. He was an Englishman, very light, and he owned an island in the Caribbean and he had a cattle ranch up in Northern California. So he was talking and he said, "You know, Louise comes from Moorea in Tahiti."

"Oh," I said, "I didn't know that." Then he said, "Yes, she's a pearl diver. She dives ninety-feet down and gets pearls."

I said, "Oh, my God, I can't believe that – that about the sharks?"

He said, "Well, their god, their Tiki, is the shark god, and they say something to him and they don't bother her clan of people, the divers."

I said, "I'd like to know what they say in case I see sharks when I go diving."

He said, "They don't tell anybody but the members of the family what particular words to say to the sharks."

I said, "Why didn't you dive?"

He said he dove into a pool of nine feet of water and he had a cold and blew his eardrums out, so he didn't dive.

Later on we found out she was one of the stars of the movie *Mutiny of the Bounty* when he met her. She wasn't the top star, but she had a good part in it and he met her on location. They got married and had a couple of children. She had a condominium on the island of Bora Bora.

It seems that at one time they didn't let tourists go to Tahiti. They made their income selling guano (bird manure) fertilizer, but then they had run out of it. The French had to get cash coming into the islands of Tahiti, so they finally allowed tourism to come in. Fortunately, I was one of the first tourists to get to go. I had a friend who was vice-president of Pan American, Charlie Greg. Robin Kincaid, the photographer, was a friend of mine as well. They knew my sister, Betty, who had been a purser on the China Clippers for Pan American. It was one of the first flights down there. I was so excited about it that the night before, I had this dream that I had missed the flight and it was a nightmare. I was so shattered. I don't think I've ever had anything excite me so much as going to Tahiti. There was an opening five days before as a result of a cancellation, and I needed a passport.

I called on my very good friend Congressman Arthur Younger and told him I needed a passport. He said he'd see what he could do. He actually got it for me in three days. So with all this pressure and my nightmare, I got to the Pan American room two hours early. They had all kinds of refreshments, including drinks. I was drinking them down and was pretty well on my way, with all the excitement. We stopped in Los Angeles and I had to go to the bathroom. I was afraid I'd lose my way and not get back to the plane. I finally made it and they woke me up about half past four in the morning and gave me some champagne and orange juice. Boy, did I have a headache! By the time we had breakfast, the sun was coming over the horizon, and there we saw Tahiti, with its beautiful green mountains and the deep blue and green of the shallow waters. It was an unbelievable sight. We landed and were greeted by the people. Wherever we went, we had to show a ticket that guaranteed we'd leave within thirty days. They wanted to be sure that nobody stayed. You had to have a round trip ticket. Whatever hotel you were in, wherever you stayed, you had to sign a chit with your passport number and all the rest. They knew exactly where you were all the time.

I went to my room at the Tahitian Hotel, and I was lying on my bed groaning with my headache when Charlie and Robin came by. They said they were getting a Tahitian pirogue, which is a Tahitian canoe, and we're going snorkeling. I grabbed my gear and off I went. I was so glad I did. We had this canoe and went out into Captain Cook's Bay. We dove down and could see forever. It was crystal clear for a couple of hundred feet. We saw fish, giant octopus – oh, it was marvelous. That night we had a celebration where the Tahitians came in and danced. I can't believe it, but there I was, dancing with a shirt and tie with these Tahitians, as was everyone else in the room. Trader Vic was with us on this excursion.

We went to Tahiti again another time, and we had planned to go to Bora Bora and then on to Makatea, which is in the Tuamotus. Then we'd go to Rangiroa and Moorea and back to Tahiti proper to Papeete. When we arrived in Bora Bora, we were taking the truck to the Bora Bora Hotel. We couldn't believe it; we saw all these boats on all the reefs. We had never seen anything like this before. We checked in and decided to take a walk down to Bloody Mary's, which is a place where we ate, to see George, the proprietor. He was a doctor, and he had flown jets, and he was a cook, and he owned this place. He had about six or eight bungalows, or Tahitian huts, that he rented out. We saw there was nothing left of the huts; they were all gone. We asked what had happened and they said there had been three hurricanes that had almost devastated the island just before we got there. The people had been sort of trapped. They couldn't get out and they were staying in the wine cellar. We went back and we took a swim before dinner.

We decided to eat at Bloody Mary's to find out what was going on. There was George with the short-wave radio and all the people there. Bloody Mary's is sort of a place where there's white sand on the floor and there's stumps of palm trees around the tables. It's very informal. In the bathrooms there are little waterfalls where you wash your hands. There are two tables the size of ping-pong tables covered with lobsters and tuna and soldier fish and parrotfish and octopus and clams, practically anything you could want. You just pick out what you want and there's a big barbecue fire in the middle and George just cooks it there for you and serves you. We were fascinated, but George was worried, and was on the phone. He said, "There's another hurricane coming down. It just knocked out Makatea."

I said, "That's where we're going."

He said, "You're not going there now. It's down, and it's just knocked out Rangiros, and it's knocked out the resort there. It's going to hit Moorea and it'll probably knock out the resort there. Then it will come and hit us in about eight or ten hours."

I said, "Whoa, I'll tell you what, George. I'll bet you $10 and an Irish coffee that it doesn't hit here."

He smiled and said, "You're on."

There was no hurricane hit. The next night we went out to dinner and George was as happy as a clam. He paid me the $10 and all the Irish coffees I could drink. What happened is that the hurricane had come down and taken a left turn and had hit Papeete and knocked out 7,000 homes, damaged hotels, tore up palm trees, and was really a mess. They don't tell you these things about the beautiful South Pacific. So here we were, we'd paid for the accommodations at Makatea and Rangiroa and the other islands, and we were stuck on Bora Bora. So we decided to make the best of it.

We had a bungalow over the water, which was beautiful. Of course the cost was about twice or three times as much as the bungalow on the beach. After about five days, which was the length of our proposed stay, we got a bungalow on the beach. It didn't have a refrigerator, but they were nice enough to haul one in and install it for us. When it came time to leave, they usually only take a couple of hundred dollars in credit cards. I said, "I'm awfully sorry," because my bill was something like 300,000 South Pacific francs. I think it was about $2,000, because the fantastic food is not included with the room. In fact, they don't include even one cup of coffee. Everything is so expensive, it is staggering. I'm happy to say that when we got back, we had refunds from all the resorts that were knocked out, and we didn't lose a nickel on the trip.

The most tragic thing that happened in Bora Bora occurred after we left. They had these giant clams that were about four or five feet long and had beautiful lips. The clams had orange polka dots and were red and green. They almost looked like snakes when they're attracting the plankton, or whatever it is that they eat. They took dynamite and blew them out of the coral there, so there were no more giant clams. Then an El Niño came along and made the water over ninety degrees and apparently the coral dies at that temperature. This gorgeous paradise… I've been trying to get them to make into a marine reserve because this is what people come to see. But they wouldn't do it. They said the Tahitians wouldn't go for it. I said that they could go out and fish and do almost anything, but they shouldn't go and destroy the reef.

One time we went to the Great Barrier Reef and flew down to Cannes and went out to a nature preserve called Lizard Island. They only allow about sixty people there at one time. You can go out thirty or forty yards and can see these giant clams and all kinds of fish. This place is 150 miles off the coast of Australia. We had to go still another fifty miles to reach the Great Barrier Reef. There was this beautiful fishing boat, and a South African gentleman named Keith and his wife said they would like to charter it, if we would charter it with them. It was a great idea. He was a certified scuba-diver. I thought that was really good, so we headed for the Great Barrier Reef.

Before I got there on the plane, the man who ran Lizard Island said, "If you're not certified, they won't give you a tank." His thought was that there was no way we could get a tank, so I would just be allowed to snorkel, not scuba-dive.

It didn't faze me, so we hopped on the boat. It was really rough. It was banging around and my wife, Jean, wasn't too happy, and said, "What about this?"

"It's a little scruffy today," he said.

So off we went. We anchored in this little place called the "Cod Hole", where the polka dot cod are. These are 200-pound fish that are white with black spots. I got on the back of the boat, and they gave me a tank with all the equipment to dive. Keith had his diving gear as well. A gentleman I thought was a dive master was with us with his tank. We were all supposed to stay together and watch each other. There are snakes, rockfish, squirrelfish, and all kinds of wild things – including, possibly, sharks.

We were out there, the only boat, and we dove in. I went down about thirty-five feet and I've never seen anything like this in my life. One of these 200-pound fish starts nibbling on my leg, and I'd have to kick him a little bit. Then I looked up and saw these green starfish and black starfish and eels and all kinds of wonderful things. When I looked around. I saw that my buddies were heading with the current. This is something you don't do, go with the current when you're fresh. You go against the current when you're fresh so when you're tired you can come back with the current. I started kicking to try to keep up with them as much as possible, and they were just scooting around. I kept my eye on them and looked out to see what was going on. I was enjoying seeing all these fish and wonderful marine life while keeping an eye on them. We were about six or eight blocks, maybe a quarter of a mile away, when all of a sudden I see them shooting up to the top. I knew something was wrong. I went up to the top and took my air out of my mouth and asked what was the matter. They had run out of air and were heading back to the boat.

Well, the waves were crashing and everything, and I knew I would never make it back to the boat if I had to go on the top. So I looked at my air and I had about 600 pounds, so I dove back down into the shallow and I'd come up and I made it back to the boat.

My wife said, "How was it?"

I said, "That's the last time I go with these ding-a-lings. They left me and I got into trouble. I'm lucky I had enough air to come back to the boat, because we were on the other side of the Great Barrier Reef."

Even though it was a foot or two over the top, the boat couldn't get over it. Anyhow, we made it. That was an experience! That didn't end it, though. Keith decided he knew everything about diving, so went to another place to do some snorkeling with our wives. His wife was an artist and had never been in the water. He decided she should jump from the ship with her fins and hold the mask against her face to make her entry. If you know what you're doing, you can do it without knocking the mask off your face. So she jumped in and she went down right to the bottom and knocked off her mask. She almost drowned. That poor woman was so shattered when we finally scooped her out! Here was this smart guy, head of a firm like the Blue Shield in the United States. They called it Blue Scene in South Africa.

The people that you meet when you're traveling and when you go to these different places are fantastic. While we were on Lizard Island, we ate breakfast or dinner with various different people. You just ate at a table, and people would come and sit down, or you'd sit with another group. So one morning these people came and sat down with us and were asking us questions about what was happening in the United States and the political deal and so forth. They said, "We're leaving and we're going into Cannes, when are you coming?"

We said, "We won't be in for a about three days."

They asked where we were staying because they said they wanted to take us on an Australian picnic. We said that would be nice, thinking that people say a lot of things that they don't really mean. Not the Australians! Three days later, before we'd unpacked our bags, the phone rang. It was our friends, and they said they were down picking up the food for the picnic. They wanted to know what we wanted, for us to come and help pick out the food, and we'll go on the picnic tomorrow.

We went out and bought two kilos, which is four pounds, of prawn. We bought wine and cheese and fruit and all kinds of stuff. They took us to some pubs and showed us what Cannes was like. The next morning at nine we hopped in the car and off we went up towards the North. This particular area is like Hawaii; the climate is very warm, humid and beautiful. We went to a national park with a stream running through it. The water was crystal clear and it had the white sand on the bottom. There were picnic tables there and cut wood if you wanted to barbecue. We had a marvelous day. I took them to dinner at our hotel after we were finished.

Parklands

We were able to increase the parks in San Mateo County, and the Board of Supervisors helped Pacifica and the State. We bought the Pacifica Beach and turned it over to the State for maintenance and operation. We bought an 800-acre piece of property for a park in Pacifica near Linda Mar. I forget what the name of it is. My contribution to that deal was that the sellers wanted $1 million for the property and we offered them $500,000. Our attorneys said that if it went to condemnation, they would probably get the $1 million. I said that the thing to do is to tell them we are not interested in it, but give them thirty days to either accept the $500,000 or we really didn't need it. By doing that, they accepted the deal. (I'm not sure what the exact time was.) My real estate background told me that no one else was going to buy that piece of property except the County. Our offer was fair, considering the value of the other property around it. They were trying to hold us up for the extra money.

Pescadero Park is a sad tale. Our genius County Manager came up with this program that we build a Pescadero dam and impound about 40,000 acre feet of water. This is a lot of water; it's enough to supply two-thirds of the needs of Marin County. The Corps of Engineers would put up the money because it could be a flood control project for the downstream area. It would create a long lake that would be used for recreation, like boating and fishing. It could be used for drinking water and irrigation along the coast. The people don't realize that the coast of San Mateo County has hardly any water whatsoever. The water they have is suspect. It is so necessary to keep the farmland. Rather than have expensive development in that area, we wanted to have people continue to raise artichokes and all kinds of things and produce dairy products. This project had four points we could sell: water, irrigation, recreation, and flood control. The Corps of Engineers looked at the project and came back and said that it would have to be 50,000 acre feet of water to make it economically feasible. In the mean time, we had arranged with the Santa Cruz Lumber Company to buy a whole park for about $50 an acre. They could take the trees where the dam was going to flood, and we would pay something low, like 25 cents per running foot for the trees left standing. That way we could keep these beautiful groves. They were very cooperative. We had this plan to put a jail down there. We would have only non-violent offenders, and they could clear and do all the grubbing of the land for the dam and use the firewood for the recreation area. A lot of thought went into the planning.

What happened was when the Corps of Engineers came up and said we needed 50,000 acre feet, that would have gone down into another park and inundated about another 125 trees. Well, the Sierra Club and the Committee for Green Foothills came down and yelled and screamed and killed the project deader than a mackerel. Here we were – we had all these trees that we were going to give Santa Cruz Lumber Company, and it would look like hell. So we had to go to the Federal government, and thank goodness McCloskey was able to get us a couple of million dollars to buy the trees. Now we have a beautiful 5,000-acre park, but Pescadero gets flooded in wet years and there's still no water for the coast.

The County has a program called "sustained yield". That means that you're growing these trees, like apricots or apples, whatever, and when the trees get old and are going to fall over, you harvest them and plant other trees. Government research went out and found that we had five to ten million dollars' worth of redwood trees that could be taken out, and the younger trees that were there could take over and have more room to grow. We would be planting more redwood trees and we would have a sustained yield and probably get five million dollars a year in the lumber business. At the same time, it would be a park, because it wouldn't be wild. We'd have more access to more areas of the park and the trees would be healthier, etc. Well, the Board of Supervisors screwed around. Next thing you know there's a big storm and it knocked down about fifteen or twenty million dollars' worth of trees that should have been harvested. I don't know if anything has happened since. These are assets that the County could utilize to reduce the cost of government. I think four million dollars would take care of the Park Department, or at least it could help.

We decided we wanted to buy the Coyote Point property. Bob Stallings, the County Manager at the time, and I went back to Washington. He was politically very astute, and he found a couple of his buddies. One of them was a Senator from the South. They both went to school at Duke University. Bob used his southern accent and told the Senator, "We'd like to get the money not only for the land, but for the land under the water." The Senator said the legislation doesn't include the land under the water. Of course, if you are talking about the Coyote Point Yacht Harbor, you had to own the land under the water. So he said again in his thick drawl, "Why Senator, you can put an endorsement on one of those bills to add that, because we need the land under the water. I know that land won't cost much, but we still need to purchase it." At that time, there was about 5,000 acres of land near there under water. It is now in Burlingame, with hotels on it. George Keaston bought it for something like $50 and acre. Then he developed a plan where surplus concrete from a demolished bridge was dumped around the outlying limits of his property. Then he got Buzz Haskins to come in and dig out the basin and fill the property. It is now full of hotels and office buildings on reclaimed land.

We received grants whereby the Federal government put up fifty per cent of the money and we matched it with fifty per cent We worked out a deal where we would give any city twenty-five per cent if they put up twenty-five per cent. This is how we got Pacifica Beach and all kinds of properties throughout the County of San Mateo. We took advantage of the largess of the Federal government.

We got involved in buying 1,000 acres of San Bruno Mountain. We bought it for open space, so that no one could build on the mountain side. There was a big development there. The owners came in with a project to develop what was called the "saddle area", and then they were going to give us the rest of the mountain. There are 3,000 acres in the mountain, ten per cent of the size of San Francisco. It went to a vote of the Board of Supervisors, but didn't pass, because they wanted to build high rises, up to fourteen stories high, on the saddle. I figured if it was just concentrated in this small area, the rest of the land could be open space. That would benefit everyone, and would not cost the County any money. But that did not happen.

I got into a free-for-all and we bought the 1,000 acres on the side of the mountain.

The conservationists and everyone wanted us to buy the saddle area. This issue went on for a long time. The conservationists got five million dollars from the State to buy it. Foremost McKesson wanted $40 million. If it went to a condemnation hearing, the State would withdraw the five million and we'd lose it. So I went to the head of Foremost McKesson Park and Land Company. His name escapes me. We chatted, and I said, "Why don't you do this? This would be the best thing, and everybody wants this particular piece of land. I know it is the most valuable piece on the whole mountain. Why don't you give it to the County or State, take the five million dollars and write off the $35 million as a gift and get a tax deal? Then if you wanted to develop some other place on the mountain, everybody would probably go for that." So they agreed, and they donated the $35 million worth and got their tax break.

The saddle area is worth $100 million today and is now a State Park controlled jointly by the County. As soon as that happened, the conservationists said they couldn't build anywhere on the mountain because of an endangered species of butterfly. The poor Foremost McKesson people, I guess, thought I sold them down the river, but I didn't know this was going to happen. They have been fighting ever since over development of the property. But through my negotiations, they did give $35 million worth of property to the State of California.

I was very friendly with Martin Wonderlich, who I have mentioned before. He had made a fortune. He loaned money to Paul Peterson of Whitecliff Homes. He backed Andy Oddstadt with Linda Mar and with the Farm Hill project in Redwood City. He bought the Folger Estate. The Folgers were the coffee people and had this beautiful estate. It had a lake on it and it had a sawmill, and the water came down from a large pipe and ran the saw that cut logs. Martin wanted to take me up and show me the mill and the stable. It had beautiful tile and he just loved the place. He showed me the meadow. We drove all over the place. Then we'd go back to his place and he'd throw these big steaks on this big oak fire. We would sit there and eat these steaks and drink his champagne and really enjoy ourselves. He always let everyone use the place before it was a park. It was his property, but the horsemen would use it, and many others. He was very generous.

One day I talked to Larry Furey, who was Martin's CPA, and asked him what if he gave this to the County as a park. He wants people to use it and he can't use it. He has his own house and thirty-five acres, which is plenty of room for him. Larry said, "Let me check it out. He could take a tax deduction for a gift."

So he checked it out, and said it was a good idea. I went to lunch with Martin and the County Manager, Marty Tarshus, and said we would like to have him donate the property to San Mateo County. Martin wasn't feeling very good, but said to check with Larry, and if Larry says it was OK, then it was OK with him. We phoned up Larry and he talked to Martin. We drew up the deeds and then Martin got really sick and it looked like he was going to pass away. He signed the deeds. Jean Fassler was chairman of the Board of Supervisors and I was the vice-chairman. She was on vacation, so I called a meeting of the Supervisors to accept the deed. We accepted the deed and it became Wonderlich Park, probably worth $200 million.

The 280 Freeway

They were developing the route for the 280 Highway extension from San Bruno to Palo Alto. The people in the Woodside area and the conservationists wanted the route to be lower, next to the lakes, and that looked like the best route. The City of San Francisco wanted the upper, or present route. The Highway District Commission thought it could save $50 million if they took the lower route. There was this big concern that if you took the lower route, you would immediately set up the lakes for development. I was called to come to the Highway Commission meeting in San Diego. When asked, I told them I thought this was one of the stumbling blocks. I suggested they buy the development rights of the Crystal Springs 25,000 acres so there would be no development on the acres containing the lakes and adjoining property. They agreed to do this, but the conservationists said that it was a sham. They talked to San Francisco's Mayor Alioto, and he came out and said that there would never be anything built on the lakes because they had passed a resolution to that effect.

Here came my real estate knowledge. Nothing like that is valid unless it is in writing on a deed and recorded. Also, one city's mayor or council cannot bind another mayor or council. That's the law, so the statement was a lot of hot air. I knew there was something involved in this, but I couldn't figure out what it was. All the politicians were for the higher route, and I was the only one against it. I was sort of on the spot when the conservationists dumped me. I thought that the lower route was what they wanted. Here there was something we could agree on, and they left me and never told me they were changing their position. I wanted the property to be signed over and dedicated. The City of San Francisco was not of that mind at the time.

I talked to Lowell Bridwell, the US Highway Commissioner, and he asked me why I was against this. I told him it was because we were not dedicating the land. He said that San Francisco had given four million dollars' worth of land to the State to have a park along the lakes. I said, "Wait a minute. They didn't give that. They *sold* it to the State for four million."

He couldn't believe that. I told him that he had to watch these guys. All I cared about was that the land on each side of the freeway was preserved as open space in perpetuity and that it was properly deeded.

The time came when Lowell Bridwell said to the whole group of us, "We're going to use this upper route, providing all the land is dedicated for open space and it cannot be changed unless the Federal government and the County of San Mateo and the City and County of San Francisco agree on the change."

Well, they almost fainted, because when 280 came through, there were 4,000 acres that would no longer be watershed. It would be on the east side of the freeway.

I guess it's worth about a billion dollars, but it's dedicated for recreational purposes. I think that's what the problem was. I really don't know, but I think that was the idea. The main thing is that I feel so good about it. I signed the agreement since I was Chairman of the Board at the time. That is going to be in perpetuity, forever, and it won't change.

Devil's Slide

Through this experience with Highway 280, I became very friendly with the Highway Commissioners. Then the City Manager of Redwood City became the Secretary of the Highway Commission. We had a terrible area, and still do, at Devil's Slide. It goes down the coast from Pacifica over to Montana. It's a dangerous road and there have been hundreds of people killed and thousands injured there by going off the side. There are slides every year, even in dry years.

The cost to maintain that road and keep it from sinking into the ocean has been enormous. I figured, Let's get this finished and let's get a good road that won't wash out. We could go over the tops of the hills in this particular area. I called up my friend the Secretary of the Highway Commission and talked to a few other commissioners, and they said, "Fine. We have $50 million, and we'll put it in that and make it a priority deal."

They went ahead and let the contract out, and just as the contractor was going to start work, a johnny-come-lately called Mrs. Meyer came in and filed a suit in the Federal court and said that there was no environmental impact study made on the Highway 1 bypass. All work was stopped, and my beautiful job of lobbying the State Highway Commission went down the drain. It came up again and the cost had gone up to over a hundred million dollars. The now Congress lady Eshoo, who was elected on the point that she would OK the bypass, has changed her mind. The environmentalists pushed her, so nothing had been done. Just the other day some fellow went off and into a ravine a hundred feet deep.

More People

Supervisor John Molinari, not Judge Molinari (his son), ran for Mayor of San Francisco. Agnos, who was mayor for four years and was defeated by Jordan, beat him. When Agnos was defeated, Willie Brown gave him a job at $110,000 a year in Sacramento. So Agnos really won, he didn't lose. The arrogance of Supervisor Molinari cost him the job of mayor. He just had that arrogance when he got into the election, and it killed him. He was a smart guy and he would probably have been a good mayor, considering the alternative.

Speaking of mayors of San Francisco, Mayor George Moscone wasn't exactly my ideal person, judging from what I read in the papers. He just didn't seem like a real nice guy. We had a problem, and San Francisco had a problem. Our problem was that we needed more water in San Mateo County for future growth. San Francisco had built a water line with four chambers. Three chambers held a huge pipe. There was one chamber that did not have a pipe, and there was room for an enormous pipe to be put in the same chamber and in the same right-of-way. So there would be no problem building it.

San Francisco had a garbage problem. They were trucking their garbage all the way up to Alameda County where all those windmills are. This was about a 115-mile round trip across the bridge. It involved thousands of tons of garbage. It was very expensive and Alameda charged them an enormous amount of money. I just felt that as an old San Franciscan, we shouldn't have hostility between San Francisco and San Mateo Counties, so I asked for a meeting with Mayor Moscone.

We met in the Mayor's office in San Francisco, which is a really elegant old office. I told him what I wanted to see him about, so he brought his staff from the Water Department to the meeting. We sat down, and I outlined basically that I was here in a cooperative program to see how we could help each other out. I said, "You have a garbage problem. We are just finishing up a big canyon site that should go to the year 2000. It's all set up, and if we took the canyon just next to it, there would be room for your garbage. However, we would have to widen the road through the watershed to Half Moon Bay so that the trucks could get through. We would ask for a fee of about five million dollars. You're paying $20 million now, so that would be a good deal for you, and for us. As far as what we want, we would like you to build another water line in that fourth chamber. I'm sure that with revenue bonds and everybody wanting more water, it would pay for itself."

He turned to his Water Department people, and they agreed, absolutely, no question, that what I said would be a benefit to everyone. We decided to get together some figures on cost and fees, etc. and study this.

Meanwhile, Dan White, a fireman who ran for San Francisco Supervisor, knew that everybody on the Board of Supervisors had another job. He thought the supervisors got about ten to twelve thousand dollars a year, and he was making $35,000 a year as a fireman, so that was what he'd like to do and it would be good. He got elected, and then he found out that you couldn't be employed in two jobs with the City and County of San Francisco. He would have to give up one of the jobs. This came as a big shock to him. Well, I think his wife was pregnant or something, and he was trying to decide. Meanwhile, everyone was going around trying to find him a job in the private sector, because he would be a swing vote on the Board, and it was important for him to remain a supervisor. Then something happened, I forget what, and he resigned from the Board. After he resigned, he changed his mind. He went to see Mayor Moscone and said, "I'd like you to reappoint me. I made a mistake, and I'd like your consideration and help on this."

Moscone said, "Let me think it over. We'll meet tomorrow at ten or eleven in the morning and I'll give you my answer."

Barbara Taylor of radio station KCBS phoned White that night. She called several times until he answered, and she was taping the call. He sounded sleepy, and she asked, "What do you think about this? Mayor Moscone is not going to reappoint you tomorrow." I don't know what happened, but he slammed down the phone. If you listen to the tape, Barbara Taylor was very upset that he treated her that way and wouldn't talk to her. The next morning he got a gun, went down and shot Mayor Moscone and Harvey Milk, another one of the supervisors. That was when Dianne Feinstein, who was President of the Board of Supervisors at the time, was selected by the Board to become mayor.

I telephoned the San Francisco water and garbage department heads, and they said, "Everything is off because now you're going to have to talk to Mayor Feinstein."

I made an appointment with her and told her what the problem was and what we had decided. I told her that we were looking into it and it was very likely that Mayor Moscone was going to go ahead with it because it was good for both of us. She sat there quietly and listened to me, never saying very much. What happened was, nothing was ever done.

Later on I went to see the County Manager of the City and County of San Francisco, Roger Boas. We had gone to Galileo High School together. I have mentioned him here before. I ran into him at our favorite restaurant, Swan's Oyster House on Polk Street, many, many times. I spoke to Roger and said, "How're things going, have you got the garbage problem solved?"

"Oh," he said, "we have a bunch of boats, and we're going to load the boats with garbage and send them down to Redwood City. They are going to burn the garbage in an incinerator and generate enough electricity to sell to the city of Redwood City."

I said, "I don't know of any incinerator that could meet the air qualifications in California." I had gone to Japan and seen their incinerators. They had a really fabulous operation for burning garbage, but checking even there, the incinerators would not meet the standards for air quality in this area.

Roger said, "There's no problem, it's all set. We've talked to the CEO of the Port Authority. Fred's all set for it."

Fred DiPietro was an old friend of mine. He lived across the street from me in Mills Park and had been one of the members of the Mills Park, Improvement Club. I phoned Fred and asked him if this was right.

He said, "Oh, yeah. We're going to build this big plant and go to town. We're going to bring in this coal from Utah because

Taiwan needs coal to run their electrical plants – same with Indonesia. We can send them this coal on the empty boats that come down here with the garbage, reloading it to the bigger boats."

I thought to myself, this is a Fantasyland. Of course, it turned out that it was a fantasy. Nothing happened, and San Francisco continued to send its garbage to Alameda.

The Last Election

I was going to run for supervisor for the sixth term. I had run five terms and was opposed only twice. On the Board of Supervisors at that time was Ed Boccaccio, who had never worked a day in his life because his father owned the California Meat Company, the land under the Transamerica Pyramid, and about fourteen different shopping centers and pieces of real estate. Also on the Board was Arlen Gregorio, who had formerly been a State Senator as well as an attorney. There was John Ward, who was a school-teacher with no business experience. There was Fred Lyons, a very poor, unsuccessful attorney. That was the Board.

I forgot a very important thing that my Dutch friend and a Councilman of the City of San Bruno told me. He said you've got to know your arithmetic. If there's a board of five people, you have to have a majority of three. If you don't have three, you will never get anything done, and you'll be completely frustrated. I missed that point completely, and I should have remembered it. Each of these people did not have the same philosophy that I had, and it showed. It was always three to two or four to one. I should have packed my bags at that time. But, I felt that I was the only one – you get goofy when you are in politics – you get a little nuts. I just thought they really needed me.

I liked the job. It wasn't that much fun as I look back. I was not that good a supervisor at that time because everything I tried to do was blocked. Yet, I didn't feel that I wanted to go back into the insurance and real estate business. I had been out of it for so long. My favorite saying is, "The future belongs to those who prepare for it." I had prepared from the time I was forty years old that all the mortgages on the property that we owned would be paid and that my pension fund would be available in about two years, so I would be in very good financial shape and I wouldn't have to worry. If I made a few real estate deals, that would be a plus. So, why I ran, I'll never know.

What happened was that Jackie Speier came into the County. She had been an aide to Congressman Leo Ryan, who was from South San Francisco. She had been an aide of his since she was seventeen or eighteen years old. They had gone up to see the seal slaughter in Canada and got a lot of good publicity on that. Leo Ryan went undercover into jail and stayed there to see what needed to be reformed in the jail system. The trouble with Leo, was that he was the nicest guy in the world; he would go on these trips, but nothing would ever come out of it. He never drew up any legislation that would correct any of the problems that he found.

He was thinking of running for Senator. He and Jackie Speier got together and he thought of this great idea. They'd get a lot of national publicity and take along some crews from NBC and others. They'd go down to Jonestown and save those 600 people there. They were supposedly all captives of this Reverend Jim Jones. So they went down and someone got frightened and shot Congressman Ryan and Jackie Speier. They killed Ryan and all of the 600 people were killed or committed suicide. It was a botched operation, you might say. Jackie Speier survived. She received about $300,000 in compensation from the Jones Temple for her medical bills, and the Federal government paid everything else.

She was looking for something to do. She didn't know where she was going to live. She went to the First District, then the Second District; she couldn't make up her mind. She was making surveys, the way you run for office now, checking on name recognition. The election was in June. I thought I had some opposition, but in April, my wife and I decided to go to Hawaii. I thought, if they want me, fine; if not, to heck with it. My God, the papers went goofy. They said, "He's gone to Hawaii. He doesn't care…" etc., etc.

At that time, it worked out well for Jackie. She had better name recognition than I did because she was shot at Jonestown. Very few people know who their supervisor is, anyhow. During the election she wasn't very nice. I did not get mean or nasty, and I am very glad about that. One of the things she hit me with, which really hurt my feelings, concerned Muriel Wonderlich. Martin Wonderlich had died, and Muriel Wonderlich was still living. We were dear friends. I had a cocktail party and I invited Muriel. It was a fund-raiser, so she sent me a check for $50 and said she couldn't come. Later in the election, I sent out a mass mailing soliciting donations, and she sent me $500. Jackie got hold of that and stated I had violated election laws because the spending limit was $500 and I got $550. I said, "My God, I forgot. I'll send the $50 back. It didn't make much difference."

Anyway, my heart and soul were not in it, and the public realized it and I lost the election.

Life After Politics

The best thing that ever happened to me was losing that election. It was sort of a shock to me. I asked myself what I was going to do now. That job had been so much fun. Then I told myself that I've got this property, and I've got my mother to take care of. My mother had been taking care of the property, and doing very well. I had an interest in it, but I hadn't been taking any money out of the investment. Then my mother got very ill.

She was living in the Marina District on Beach Street when she got sick. I had to have six nurses in to take care of her. Twenty-four-hour care takes three nurses for five days and another three nurses for the weekends and holidays. It ended up costing me about $75,000 for the nurses; plus, I was feeding them. I thought, Gee, I have to raise the income from the property.

I sent out a letter to the six tenants there and said that I wanted to paint the building and I was going to raise the security deposits from $100 to $200. There was rent control in the City, and the tenants got mad and went to the Rent Control Board and said I was going to gouge them. They went to the other building that we had on Beach and Divisadero Streets and got the tenants there to form a tenants' union against me. I always thought that I treated them pretty well. The tenants on Beach Street were paying about $500 to $700 a month. They were getting 1500 square feet of living space, doweled maple floors, two bathrooms, kitchen, dinette, dining room, and living room. Plus, we paid all the electricity. They didn't care if they left the lights on all night or not. I changed the system so there were individual electric meters and they went along with that. It was a very elegant piece of property. One of the units that was empty and not covered by the rent control rented out at $2,500 a month, the market value at that time. I felt they were not being fair.

I always like people to be fair, because I like to be fair with people. I got angry and decided I'd make condominiums out of the place. I got everything in order and got my permits for the condominium conversion. I checked with an attorney and wrote letters to the tenants offering to sell them their units for $125,000. They had ninety days to decide. If they didn't wish to buy, they would be asked to move at the end of the year. They laughed and thought it was ridiculous. The year passed. After a lot of commotion, they moved. Then I offered it for sale at $200,000 per unit. So they had an opportunity to get a real good deal. It had been bringing me a gross of $10,000, and I was able to trade this for fifteen units in Tiburon, which was bringing in twenty times that amount of money. The resale on those units went for $375,000 with a little minor improving.

I started to have enough money to care for my mother, which was critically important to me. She became very ill and attacked one of her nurses. The doctor said it would be better to put her into a nursing home, which she wanted as well.

I thought I had made a marvelous deal trading the property on Beach for the Tiburon property, and the income was much better. My sister had died, and she had two boys and a girl. I had taken them in on the deal with me. They had about twenty-five per cent interest in it. I took them over proudly to see the property in Tiburon. My niece, Simone, said, "This place is the shits!"

I was shattered. I said, "Don't you realize that the income here is much better? There'll be more money to take care of your grandmother."

She said, "I don't want to do this. I wanted one of those condominiums for myself."

I didn't say anything, but I thought to myself, That's too bad. That's the way life goes.

Next, I decided to focus my attention on 3701 Divisadero Street. I cleaned it up, painted it, put on a new roof, and got an interior designer to put new chandeliers in the lobby and on the outside. I did about as much as I could do with the property. My mother passed away, and we had to divide the property up. I wanted the nephews and nieces to stay in the property so they would have an income. But they didn't want that, they wanted cash. I told them then that they could have the building at 3701. It was appraised at $1,400,000. If they wanted to sell it, they could get $1,800,000 or something like that. No way, they just wanted cash. Well, I thought they'd stick me with the capital gains and income taxes. We thrashed it around. I couldn't get the price they wanted for the selling of the property, but I couldn't buy them out unless I did sell the property. I was ready to go on a cruise from Barcelona to Venice, so this was a very inconvenient time right then.

I didn't want to put the property up for sale, because I couldn't tell anybody what the price would be. I knew three real estate people, and one of them had bought a piece of property from us about fifteen years before. I phoned him to ask if he was interested in the property. He certainly was. He came over and looked at it and asked how much it was going for. I said I didn't have a price, but he said if I let him know what the price is, we'd work out a deal. I thought I'd try to do that. Another friend offered me about $1,400,000 for it. I told him I didn't think that would be enough. We needed probably about $1,800,000. I talked to an attorney, and he said if I got that amount we could close everything out. This was about seven or eight days before we were to start our trip. The attorney called back and told me they had accepted my offer.

I said, "What do you mean, 'accepted my offer'?"

"They'll accept the $1,800,000 cash," he said.

I said, "I haven't sold the property yet."

"Well," he said, "I'm sorry, but you told me that you would give $1,800,000."

"No," I said, "I said I think I can *sell* the property for $1,800,000."

"Sorry," he said, "you put me in a bind, and I have to hold you responsible for $1,800,000."

I phoned the first guy, Carlos, and he wasn't around. Couldn't find him, he was away for four days. This was Thursday. We were leaving Tuesday. There was another real estate person, Arthur, who had said he was interested. I was going to a baseball game with my brother-in-law and everybody else, and we were going to go out to dinner. I was so nervous thinking I was in real hot water. It was 5:15, and I phoned up Arthur to see if he was interested. He had never seen the place. His office said that he had left. Oh my God!

"Is there any way I can get him?" I asked. They gave me his cellular number and I phoned him. "Arthur, this is Jim Fitzgerald. You're interested in my property on Beach and Divisadero in the Marina?"

He said, "Oh, yeah. I'm interested in that."

I said, "How interested?"

He said, "Very interested. You be in my office tomorrow at 1 P.M. I'd like to make a deal on that."

I said to myself that I couldn't believe this. I had been in the real estate business fifty years and never heard of this happening. I said, "OK, I'll be in your office."

So I go to his office and he said, "What's the price?" I said, "$1,800,000." He's got the papers all made up, $1,800,000. I told him I didn't own all this property, but I would sign the agreement as an agent. He was agreeable to that. He offered to put up $5,000, but I told him he needed to put up $20,000. Well, he didn't have $20,000, so I told him to write out a check for it. I wouldn't cash it, but he needed to put more than that on it. Then I went home wondering what I was going to do because of the other quasi-commitment I had made.

I phoned Zanelo, the first guy who I was supposed to see Monday. I looked at the papers and I felt I had almost confirmed this deal. So I sent Zanelo a telegram saying, "I'm sorry but I have sold the property."

Well, on Monday this guy's chasing me all over town. I think he's going to kill me. I'm hiding. I jump on the boat and I'm off to Europe!

When I came back I closed the deal with this fella who was a 40-year-old real estate man as well as a real estate attorney. About seven months later the place burned down. This was the building destroyed in the 1989 earthquake. We had about $2,000,000 worth of insurance, including earthquake coverage. I had offered to have him take over the earthquake policy, but he didn't want it. The place burned down. One person died. It was not one of my tenants. It was one of his. Many people were injured. It cost him $4,500,000 to rebuild. There were twenty-one units on the property originally, and all he could get rebuilt on the property was fifteen. He sold the units for about $325,000 each.

So, getting knocked off the Board of Supervisors was an excellent thing for me. I had the opportunity to get my own financial situation in shape.

The Fitzgerald Family Business, which is apartment houses, has had a long history, as you can see. My father, James V. Fitzgerald, went into the real estate business in 1912 and I joined the firm in 1940. The first acquisition, as I explained before, was a 21-unit place at 3701 Divisadero. The second place was 2235 Beach Street. The third was the property at 25th and Mission Streets in about 1940-41. In 1959, Alfred Hansen, of Max Hansen & Son, went into a partnership with me to build the Crestview Properties. This was thirty units on 2201 and 2221 Princeton. Later on, we made the 2235 Beach Street properties into condominiums. We exchanged seven of them for a 15-unit building in Tiburon. We then sold 2235 Beach. We sold 3701 Divisadero to take care of the estate taxes of Gladys Fitzgerald and to buy out Burnett Miller, Simone Miller and Fitzgerald Miller. They are my sister's children and had been included as part of my sister's estate. We sold Mission Street because my partner wanted to sell. I was in political office as County Supervisor in San Mateo County at the time. It was against my principles to make a real estate deal during this period. He then received a good offer from another person. Much as I disliked selling the property, I felt it was the only way to do it. As long as I didn't want to buy it, I should not be a dog in the manger and stop the sale. As it stands today, the family business is an interest in the thirty units at 2201 and 2221 Princeton and nineteen at 23 Circle Drive in Tiburon.

One of the tragedies earlier in our life happened when Jean's mother, Gladys, and her father, Chris, went up to see Gladys's uncle. On the way back, they were going through Vallejo. A car full of mourners from an Italian funeral crossed the double line and ran into Jean's father's car. Jean's father, mother and uncle were all in the front seat. Her mother was killed and the uncle was smashed up, and so was Jean's father. That was a big blow to the family. The only reason Chris and Jean's uncle survived was because it was a very big Cadillac and it protected them in some way. This uncle was deaf. One day he went out to close the gate or something outside and got stuck. They lived out in the country. His sister was also deaf. She couldn't hear him call out, and he died.

When Jean and I first got married, we went up to see Aunt Kate, my father's sister. She lived on Pacific Avenue in an old three-story, piece of property. It was a very elegant house in the San Francisco style. When we got there, Aunt Kate asked Jean if she wanted Aunt Kate to read the tea leaves and her palm. Jean agreed. Aunt Kate would do this to my father, and my father thought that she was a witch, because when she told his fortune, he thought it actually came true, what she said. The way she said it and the way he interpreted it afterwards made it seem like what she predicted happened.

In this case, Aunt Kate looked at Jean's palm and read the tea leaves and said that Jean's hands were not meant for hard work, and that she was going to travel extensively. The most interesting thing is that Jean did not work. She worked very hard as a wife and mother, but did not work more than four years in the business world. We have traveled extensively all over the world. So, her prediction really did come true.

Aunt Kate was an interesting person. She read a book a day. She didn't do any work. She had a rooming house and there was Uncle Brewster, Brewster Frost Ames. Apparently the Frosts came over on the *Mayflower*, which was a long time ago. He spoke nine different languages. After Aunt Kate died, he studied Chinese, because he already spoke Greek, Spanish, Latin, German, French and whatever. There was a big picture of him in the paper when he was eighty-seven. He was then going to school in Chico, and he was dancing. He was a perpetual scholar.

I didn't like him at first. I thought he was a pain in the butt, but after I got to know him, I really appreciated what an intelligent and great guy he was. I'm sorry that I was not sophisticated enough when I was younger to appreciate him as much as I do now.

Aunt Kate was an interesting person. She wrote a book when she was seventy-three. I figured that if she could write a book at seventy-three, I could write a history of the family and some of the experiences I have been fortunate enough to have.

Jim and Jean – Present Day

Light suit Bob St. Clair – Hall of Fame

James V. Fitzgerald, Jr.

Mayor of San Bruno
1952–1960

James Fitzgerald was elected to the San Bruno City Council in 1952. He says that the reason he ran for the office was just to get a chance to practice public speaking. Shortly after he joined the Council, there was a power struggle between the two established political factions. The mayor resigned. In an "executive session" in a back room, the senior members of the Council declined to serve as mayor, so Jim was selected.

It was assumed that the usual power brokers would continue to run things, as the job of mayor at that time was mainly ceremonial. Jim discovered that his one bit of power was that of appointing Commissioners. He exercised that power judiciously, and found that he was, in fact, able to influence matters in San Bruno. By reassigning the Commissions among the other Council Members, he was able to shift some of the power. This caused newspaper headlines that read, "Fitzgerald Takes Over". He also joined with the mayors of other peninsula cities to address some of their common problems.

During Jim's tenure as mayor, San Bruno built several new civic buildings. Fitzgerald is proud of the fact that they were able to "pay as you go" for these projects without having the city go into debt.

In 1953, a new City Hall was opened. The cost, paid in cash, was a little over $300,000.

A year later, a new main library was built for $150,000. Selling the old library property to the Bank of America funded this project. With the proceeds of the sale, the new library could be built on land already owned by the city.

When a community center was needed, cash on hand was sufficient only to start the project. It was built in two stages, the first for cash and the second financed by a special two-year tax. The second portion was not built until the funds were available to complete it.

A city swimming pool was also added in 1959, funded by "contributions" from the contractors developing San Bruno. Jim admits that a tax on the newly developed lots would not have been legal, but he convinced the builders that it was not fair of them to come into San Bruno without making a contribution. A children's library was also built for $9,000 from this fund.

A bond issue was needed to fund improvements in fire protection. It took two ballots before it passed, but it resulted in the construction of three new firehouses as well as new trucks and equipment.

Parking around San Mateo Avenue became a problem. Jim describes this as one of the most horrible experiences of his life. In order to provide parking, it was necessary to condemn some houses in the area. The amount of the compensation was not enough to allow the owners to buy new homes of equal value. Jim tried to increase the amount that they were to receive, but that was not legally possible. The business owners along San Mateo Avenue paid for the cost of the parking lot.

As San Bruno was growing, Fitzgerald was able to negotiate with the developers to provide the city with parkland and public works improvements as part of the new construction. Jim had originally been in the real estate business, and his expertise in this area benefited the city of San Bruno.

Andres Oddstadt was a developer who was building housing on the coast in today's Pacifica. He was working in an area called Linda Mar, and found he couldn't get enough water to supply the development. He approached Jim to ask if he could buy water from San Bruno. San Bruno got its water from San Francisco's Hetch Hetchy system. There were restrictions on San Francisco selling water to private parties, but no problem in San Bruno reselling it. Fitzgerald struck a deal whereby Oddstadt would build the needed pipeline and water tank, and then pay 15% to San Bruno for brokering the water. This provided additional income to the city. When the mayor and Oddstadt began to talk about cutting a road over the hills between the communities, people on the coast worried that San Bruno was about to annex them. The City of Pacifica incorporated in order to prevent this.

Development in San Bruno took place in the Crestmoor Park and Rollingwood area. It was very rainy during those years, and with the tree removal that had been done for the construction, mud was sliding down the hills. Fitzgerald insisted that they plant replacement trees and donate San Bruno Park to the city. Martin Wonderlich was one of the partners in this development, and from this a close friendship developed between Wonderlich and Fitzgerald.

When The San Francisco International Airport was expanding, they were hauling hundreds of tons of dirt along San Bruno Avenue. The huge trucks were tearing up the street and the hours of operation, starting at 5 A.M. were upsetting the residents. Jim arranged with the Teamsters Union to start work later, but his efforts to get the City of San Francisco to pay for the damage to the street were unsuccessful. Jim initiated a program of stopping every third truck along the street to inspect the breaks, etc. San Francisco then agreed to pay 2 cents a ton into a trust fund to fix San Bruno Avenue.

After serving as mayor for San Bruno, Jim Fitzgerald decided he enjoyed the excitement of politics, and he decided to run for the San Mateo County Board of Supervisors. He ran against Tom Callan, a local developer who had served for several ballots. Traditionally absentee ballots favored the incumbent, so Jim and his wife, Jean, left for Carmel for a much needed vacation after the campaign. Five or six days later, all ballots were counted and Jim found that he had won the election by about 500 votes. He remained on the board for about twenty years, and served as President of the Board for five terms. During that time, he was involved in many projects dealing with health, safety and public works. Again, his experience from the real estate business proved very valuable. His most enduring legacy, possibly, will be in the public parks that were developed due to his interest.

Parks and Open Space

A copy of a document follows which list the Park Acquisitions and Development during Jim's years on the Board. His personal involvement accounted for many of these improvements. Jim complains that the press unfairly labeled him as a person who wanted to cover the county with homes and development. The only developments that he says he voted for were for moderate housing, while by contrast, he was instrumental in obtaining thousands of acres in Parkland and Open Space.

In 1969, as President of the County Board of Supervisors, Jim Fitzgerald led in the designating of the Moss Beach tide pool area as a Marine Reserve. It was very controversial at the time, as teachers and preservationists came in opposition with sports fishing and scuba-diving organizations. Clippings in the collection that follow explain some of the issues that were involved. The State of California upheld the reserve status, and it was named the James V. Fitzgerald Marine Reserve in Jim's honor.

Wonderlich Park is made up of 934 acres donated in 1974 by Mr. & Mrs. Martin Wonderlich to the County. The Wonderlichs had always been generous about sharing that beautiful property from the old Folger Estate with the public. They were friends of Jim's, and he is the one who suggested that they donate the property as a park. A developer was interested in buying the land, but there were no water or sewer connections. Jim pointed out the tax advantages of giving the property to the County, and Wonderlich Park was established.

Development on San Bruno Mountain was another controversy of the 1970s. Specifically, the 330-acre saddle area of the mountain was the focus of the debate. Residents wanted it preserved as open space, but developers saw it as the prime piece of real estate property. The State had allocated funds to purchase part of the land for a State Park, but the amount was insufficient to pay for the land in question. Fitzgerald was able to convince the developer, Foremost McKesson, of the tax benefit for donating part of the land in addition to the State money that paid for some of the rest. A deal was struck in 1979, and San Bruno State Park came into being.

State Highway 280 extends through the watershed of the Crystal Springs Reservoir. The City of San Francisco presented a motion declaring the watershed open space. When the highway was being proposed, two routes were considered. The upper route would have required more grading and costlier construction. The Sierra Club initially favored a lower route, but they suddenly changed their position and backed the upper design. The Sierra Club wanted the watershed as open space. Jim advised the California State Highway Commission to buy the development rights. It would not be expensive due to the resolution by San Francisco. Since a later Board could reverse a resolution by the city, Jim insisted that it be dedicated by a recorded deed. San Francisco objected, but through Jim's insistence, the Highway Director held for the deed of the property.

As a result of the highway route, 8,000 acres on the east side were no longer watershed property and could have been sold for development. This area was designated to be recreational area. The Sierra Club wanted the County to buy it for Edgewood Park, and indicated a golf course could be built there. Jim voted against a park this time, as he felt that the Sierra Club had no intention of allowing a golf course or other recreational development. The park was approved, 4 to 1 over his objection. That was over twenty-five years ago, and there is still no golf course. The park is usable to the public only for hiking, biking and horseback riding.

Although now retired, Jim Fitzgerald still remains vitally interested in the ecology of the peninsula. His concerns for more recent activities, especially the partial closures of some County Parks are reflected in some of the letters and clipping that follow.

Health and Safety

As a freshman member of the Board of Supervisors, Jim was appointed to be the Civil Defense and Disaster Chief. There was no Civil Defense Program and there had been no disasters in recent years, so the job really had no function. The Cold War was just heating up, and people began asking questions about the County's plans. Jim realized that it was time to develop a program that could at least handle local problems. At about that same time, Jim received a call from the Sheriff one night. It had been raining hard, and the Sheriff asked that the National Guard be called out as Pacifica was flooded and looting was going on. Jim called the Governor and got the needed help. In the morning he called out the County Engineer and got the mess cleaned up. At the next Board meeting he was informed that he did not have the authority to spend money as he had done. Citing his responsibility as Disaster Chief, Jim got the Board to pass a resolution providing him access to a fund for such purposes.

The only way to coordinate disaster relief was to have the twenty cities in the County cooperate. Jim got monthly meetings going to coordinate all the law enforcement, fire and public works departments of all the cities and the County. Due to the dedication of the participating mayors and councilmen, the County Disaster Board became a great agency.

During his years as supervisor, Jim served as President of the San Mateo County's Comprehensive Health *Planning* Council, Vice-Chairman of the Bay Area Comprehensive Health Planning Council, and President of the Health Service Agency for the United States for San Francisco, Marin and San Mateo Counties. He was also director of a consortium for better coordination among the six hospitals in San Mateo County.

Fitzgerald was the driving force in the Joint Powers Agreement for the County wide 911 Emergency Health Medivac Service that started in 1976. In his honor, the James V. Fitzgerald

Award is presented each year by the Peninsula Emergency Services Association to recognize an outstanding emergency program.

Intergovernmental and Fiscal Matters

In his years with the Board, Jim served on many committees and boards dealing with intergovernmental relations. His role was always to seek compromise and cooperation between peninsula cities or governmental agencies. He maintained a reputation for being a fiscal conservative, while being innovative with his cost-saving ideas.

One of Jim's first projects on the Board of Supervisors was to cut costs through eliminating redundant government services on the peninsula utilizing a city-county coordinating committee. In one incident, he proposed shifting the responsibility of fire protection in county watershed areas to the California Department of Forestry. This represented a saving to the county of at least $160,000 per year and conformed to the way other counties did it.

A new courthouse in South San Francisco was needed, and Jim proposed using the recently designed plans for the San Mateo courthouse with a few modifications. This eliminated the expense of drawing new plans for a similar facility. As a result, a larger facility was possible at less cost than a smaller project started from scratch.

As a board member of the North County Sanitation District, Jim proposed the reclaiming of effluent for use as irrigation water for the cemeteries and golf courses. This would have created an income source and conserved water during drought. Unfortunately, Jim was not successful in overcoming public aversion to the idea, and the plan was not implemented.

Other Matters

In 1972, an auto was reported stolen by a woman in East Palo Alto. The Sheriff's Officers were making out their report when the woman recognized her car going by. She told the Officers, and they pursued the auto. The car stopped and the two occupants ran. The Officers ordered them to stop, but they kept going. An Officer fired at one of the men, hitting him in the shoulder. Unfortunately, the bullet traveled up to the perpetrator's head, killing him. It was later found that the suspect had just been released from jail.

After the incident, members of the community came to Jim demanding that the Officer be charged with murder. In his usual blunt way, Jim told them that if you steal a car, that was a chance you took. Reaction to this statement was immediately very vocal, and as a result, Jim was issued a revolver and provided with bodyguards.

In an attempt to resolve the issue, Jim met with the community activists. They insisted that a park be named in honor of the deceased suspect. They claimed that this was the view of the entire community. Jim assented, asking only that they put it to a vote and they agreed to that. The voters of East Palo Alto turned it down. While not a "politically correct" response to the incident, three letters of support follow.

Over the years, Jim Fitzgerald has battled with the Sierra Club several times over various projects. He feels that they have cost the County millions of dollars and the loss of parkland. Three specific cases he cites are:

The controversy over the San Bruno Mountain development: Jim feels that the endangered butterfly would have had 2,000 acres to roam if they had not objected to the development of 250 acres. Now, due to lack of visitors and budget constraints, the park has had to restrict its hours.

Lack of water has always been a problem to the farmers on the coast: a plan was developed to stop the periodic flooding of Pescadero Creek by building a dam. This would have controlled the flooding, created a reservoir for needed irrigation water, and resulted in a recreational lake and park. The U.S. Corps of Engineers would have paid for the project. The Sierra Club killed the project through its opposition. Water is still a problem and Pescadero Creek still floods.

Highway 1, Devil's Slide bypass: thirty years ago, a scenic, four-lane highway was proposed for forty million dollars, but was opposed by the Sierra Club. Now, after the loss of many more lives and costly road closures, the Sierra Club has approved the plan for a tunnel that will cost 275 million dollars. They say this is saving the environment. Jim wonders where they are going to put the dirt from the tunnel. Some recent letters Jim wrote are included in this scrapbook. Interestingly, they indicate that he has become a member of the organization himself.

In 1980, Jim was opposed in re-election to his sixth term by Jackie Speier. She had become very well known in the aftermath of the Jonestown Massacre in which Leo Ryan, among so many others, was killed, and she was seriously injured. Ms. Speier defeated Jim, and for the first time in years he found himself with time to pursue his own interests.

Jim's mother was ailing. He was able to spend more time with her and attend to her final needs without distraction.

Jim had refrained from dealing in real estate during his years in politics because he saw in it the possibility of appearing as a conflict of interest. Now he was free to redirect his and his family's investments. As a result, he sold an apartment building in the Marina district of San Francisco in 1989. Seven months later, the Lorna Prieta earthquake hit, and that was one of the buildings that burned down. One person was killed. Jim had fire and earthquake insurance on the property when he owned it and offered to have the new owner take the policy over, but he had declined.